I Live to Laugh, Thus I Let Go

MORHAF AL ACHKAR, MD, PH.D.

Printed in the United States.

Cover and book design by Asya Blue Design.

ISBN 9798847989541 Paperback
ISBN 9798354871575 Hardcover

To NaKaisha

Table of Contents

•

In the place of an introduction 1

Life as experiences 11

    Examples of experiences 17

    From describing to modifying 22

    Practice, practice, and practice more! 25

    Changing experiences toward something 27

Laughing 31

    We laugh to heal 36

    We laugh to love 38

    We laugh to not cry 41

    Living to laugh is an existential decision 45

    What is laughter? 49

    How to laugh 57

    Laughing anytime at anything 62

    Laughing with style 65

    What stops me from laughing? 69

Letting go is liberation 73

    Letting go with grace 80

    How to let go by laughing 83

    Letting go with laughter is liberation 93

    Planning to laugh and let go 95

Letting go of letting go 97

In the place of an introduction

I lived for the significant part of the past five years with the expectation that my chance of surviving five years would be close to 1 in 20. If you look up the prognosis for stage IV lung cancer, you will find those statistics and even worse. Although I was fortunate to respond to my novel chemotherapy, and my prognosis is better than average considering my age and other factors, the looming thought of the end of my life haunted me.

Shortly after my cancer diagnosis, I busied myself finishing all the projects I had launched, not wanting to leave any loose ends. I completed my PhD and published a few papers that had been on the shelf for a while. I also read a lot of philosophy, trying to find a "Final Answer," and visited with people who wanted to say goodbye. Yet, I kept waking up alive. When I set out to meet other people who, like me, were living with advanced-stage lung cancer, I quickly discovered that I wasn't the only one. I was motivated to learn from others in my situation and see how they found meaning and became resilient, despite living with a health condition that threatened to shorten their lifespan. I interviewed 40 patients and wrote my first book on meaning and resilience. In the process, I found a sense of purpose through my work and also learned how to become more resilient.

However, I was getting weighed down by my cancer diagnosis and the reality of living with it every day. I was also tired of striving to find meaning and resilience. I missed me, the old me. That's why I wrote my memoir, *Being Authentic*, to reconstruct my identity as a person. I am much more than my cancer; I have infinite aspects to my identity. I wanted to find my authentic self and rebuild that self to move on with living life, participating in what I called "our" project—humanity.

After writing my memoir, I discovered that there is something as important as being authentic to oneself: being there for others with love. I've had the experience of receiving acts of love, and I wanted to learn how to live my life extending love to others. I realized that if I died soon, I would leave everything I have to others. I wanted to live with love in the sense of giving others what I have while I'm still alive. But because others are unlikely to accept my gifts unless they're meaningful to them, I developed this notion of love being those actions that prioritize the other person's needs and wants. Therefore, I have advocated for putting one's feelings to the side and thinking instead of love as an action.

Even before publishing my book, *A Love Attempt*, I recognized the need for something else that's more foundational, at least from an existential standpoint. Yes, even more foundational than love! I realized that to love, you need *another person* to love, and that may not be attainable all the time. For some, it may never happen. My fear of dying alone overwhelmed me. I was also afraid that as I encountered love and opened myself up to being vulnerable, I would hurt so badly that it would be impossible for me to heal. But I found the antidote: laughter! I became obsessed with laughing. I was learning about love and practicing my attempts at love, but early on, I knew I needed laughter to survive the journey I was on. This was the something I knew I was missing.

I bounced around the idea of learning how to laugh with friends, thinking about what makes people laugh. I also thought about the physiological function of laughing in the sense of muscles moving and air pushing in and out of the lungs. I tried to learn how humor works, too. But before I fully developed my ideas on the subject of laughing, I fell in love. When you approach others with love, love happens!

It was the first time in my adult life that I was able to be fully present and give my whole self to a meaningful connection with a beloved person. My journey with meaning and authenticity had set me on a path of healing my many wounds; my awareness of my finitude with cancer allowed me to appreciate the special connection I had found; and my framework of love as action allowed me to participate and give fully in the relationship. I developed a strong and deep attachment that was so all-encompassing that when the romance ended, I was shattered.

I loved this woman so much that I couldn't get enough of us together and never wanted anything or anyone else. After publishing my work on resiliency, authenticity, and love, I felt that I had paid my dues in this world. I had an established career and was developing my ambitions more every day. I was coming to a place of peace with where I was, and all I wanted in my life was to love. I was fully in the relationship, but my partner decided she only wanted to be in my life as a friend, not as a lover. So she broke up with me.

The breakup caused me to contemplate ending my life. As a cancer patient, thoughts of death had often crossed my mind. I was determined to end my life with dignity after having suffered so much and continuing to suffer, both physically and mentally. I was battling to stay alive, but my life after the loss of this relationship became one of such daily misery that the prospect of stopping the fight was tempting.

I am scribbling these words down, so I obviously did not end my life. Instead, I decided to distract myself by going out into the world and seeking a new connection. I slipped back into the dating scene. Quickly, I met a person who was ready to form a relationship, and within a week, I felt that she had developed an attachment to me. However, I wasn't ready at all, and I felt that this difference in the desired speed of the relationship and level of interest was a burden. This led me to empathize with my ex's position—and I laughed at the absurdity of life. Previously, I had been ready and developed a strong attachment to someone who was not available to accept my love. Then, I became the object of someone's romantic interest; she was ready to build a connection with me, but I wasn't with her. The irony of the situation reminded me of my old project about laughter, so I started writing about it again to wrangle back some control over my life.

The loss of the bond with the woman I loved triggered in me the deeper existential question about living and dying. I made the link between the loss of my romantic love and my fear of death. I do not want to die alone. This has been an essential part of my torment. I am extremely afraid of dying, especially dying alone. That's precisely why I needed to laugh.

After a few weeks of back and forth, trying to salvage the love relationship, I discovered that I had a choice. I could let her go with grace or keep on struggling. I realized that I had acted foolishly in some of my desperate attempts to win her back. I loved her as a person, and she was still that person. It's true that she didn't want a romantic relationship, and she was entitled to that choice. When I told other people who were interested in me that I didn't want a relationship, they chose to not have me in their lives. Many wanted a relationship but not me as a person. What I genuinely wanted was the person who was my ex, even though I no longer had a romantic bond with her. So I let go, and I laughed.

I truly believe that laughing is a core response to our existential struggle. Exploring laughter deeply and making it an integral element of my life project are tasks worthy of my time, especially if my life will be cut short. Even if I am fortunate to live longer, these tasks still need to be done now. I have encountered hardship and consider it an inevitable part of our lived human experience. I am grateful that I have a job, home, education, and "stable" health. However, I have suffered in my life, as we all have on different levels. I define suffering as that discomfort or aching when encountering conditions, occurrences, or changes that are beyond what one can comfortably manage on a day-to-day basis. Of course, one can always choose to not challenge oneself and, thus, may struggle less. However, because I seek to experience life fully, life will confront me with difficulties. We also do not choose to get sick. We suffer by virtue of being living human beings.

The main goal of this work is not to teach someone how to be funny: it is to learn to laugh and let go. I do believe people can learn to develop their sense of humor, and that is certainly relevant to the goal of the book. It takes practice, though. It also takes practice in developing empathy in order to be mindful of others so that you do not hurt them while you're "healing." This book is also not about being funny in the sense of entertaining and amusing others. It's about people laughing, whether alone or with others.

This book is for everyone who wants to carry on living, whether they have encountered a loss, plan to take a risk, or are challenging themselves with a task. We need to laugh along the way; we need to laugh to heal; we need to laugh to keep going. Life requires that we give it 150 percent. And it's within our capacity to give to this degree! But that means we must free ourselves from whatever weighs us down. We need to laugh to lighten our loads. We will undoubtedly fall along the way and struggle to get back up. We need to train ourselves to stay up and prepare for worse things to happen. To endure and be ready for life's unexpected challenges, we must empty a space in our souls. That's where letting go is essential.

The intent of this book is to help you set up a framework to live and laugh. It will give you the tools you need to revise some of your foundational positions while providing exercises to help you build a new framework to replace the old one. The goal is to establish a new system of ideas and ground these within the structures of your mind. Importantly, this book will help you develop the tools that will enable you to reflect on your experiences and learning as you go through life.

To write this book, I sat down with the experiences I was going through and endeavored to describe their elements. I put to words the feelings I was encountering. I also reflected on my frameworks for understanding what was happening. I processed what I had gone through, and then I made explicit how I had responded to these challenges in order to share this with others. When I put together the steps I took to achieve a task, I refined them along the way. I moved back and forth between my experiences, my understanding of them, and my work on them using the tools I am developing.

You might call this project a self-development book. I dislike the term "self-help," but you can call it that if you want. Maybe it's not so bad after all since everyone needs help. My hope is that others will find my stories and reflections useful for their development. I think we can benefit from the steps others have taken in facing a particular challenge or task by practicing them on our own.

I am developing my ideas for this book within a system that I developed in my previous three books. The challenge with this project, however, is that it uses humor. With humor, you approach an idea or a concept lightly. You create distance between yourself and committing to the idea. It's saying and not saying at the same time. When you laugh at something, you break away from a certain constriction and allow yourself be free of it. This philosophical system that includes humor is unusual and offbeat. It does not need a beginning or end; it can meander wherever it wants. It will be disrupted and disrupting. It will be in places of discomfort that are managed with lighthearted laughter. The flexibility in this project is what most excites me most about it. I can do with it whatever I want and laugh along the way. I can let go of being too methodical, and I can give myself some slack.

Part of me wants to develop a masterpiece that can stand next to other important works in a library. However, if I want to do this work with authenticity, I must accept that it may turn out to be a turd in the eyes of readers and those who will decide on the value of the work. I oscillate in my desire between being disciplined and contained within a flow that makes sense to me and potential others and giving up my urge for methodical exploration. After all, why do I need to be systematic when exploring the topic of humor? I want to have fun with this work. I see humor as random, not systematic. Yes, you might have a style where you can come up with jokes like a machine. But laughter and good humor shatter the predictable and come as a surprise. Like that release after a person holds their breath for a minute, humor releases anxiety and nervousness.

This book attempts to link two elements in an existential position: I live to laugh; I laugh to let go. These are two foundational claims that will establish the sets of actions and positions outlined in this book. Although I will speak about laughing as a function and about letting go as a simple task, I refer to them here as high-level attitudinal stances. This is a difference, for example, between saying, "I am giving you this or that" and "I live to give." There is also a difference between "I am allowing this to happen" and "I choose to say yes." Laughing and letting go are fundamental choices that are grounded in adopting certain attitudes. They are the stances we take in life.

To me, laughing means hovering at the limit of rationality and letting go of what appears sane, even if for just a little while. I have wanted to take on this challenge of exploring the limits of rationality for a few years but didn't have the tools. Letting go as a radical choice is being able to say, "I'm flirting with a radical doubt because today, I will let go of what I consider true, right, and authentic." It also means making light of what one considers important or of value. It is taking a break from certainty and faith. Through humor, people can say things they don't necessarily mean, or maybe they do, at least partially.

The book does not intend to introduce a radical nihilism about life or merely cackle at the absurdity of our existence. The opposite is true: this book is about engaging with life fully. I will introduce a framework for recultivating yourself, but this will require some work to set the stage. You will need to let go of this, let go of that. You will laugh along the way to stay whole. Then, you will let go of your letting go. You will develop a new self with new positions. With the choice to let go, you are leaving behind what you have considered rational. I also wrote this book partly to develop a strategy that will help protect me against violence. I have encountered violence on the street in the way people look at me as an immigrant. I have encountered it in acts of prejudice. I've also experienced it in my internalized views of how others view me.

I want to be able to push back and laugh at what I encounter so that I can stay whole.

Life as experiences

It's been almost 40 years since I first saw the light of this world, and I'm not confident I have known all these years how to live life. Yes, I have heard words of wisdom about how to do this or that in a certain way and how to act. But no one taught me much about living, at least not in a way that really stuck. It's not anyone's fault. Learning how to live wasn't included in the school curriculum, let alone at home or on the streets. No one will give you a useful, straight answer. They typically just tell you what they're doing in their own lives and say that you'll have to find your own way. Those responses are from open-minded, thoughtful individuals who can see differences and accept them. There are also the religious fanatics who give you sets of instructions that come from what they (and often not you!) consider the Holy of Holies. The first type of answers doesn't help me much, and the second ones annoy me a lot. Over the years, I have become weary of the religious group's nonanswers to life's problems. In reality, they cause tremendous damage.

Put yourself in my shoes. After surviving five years with stage IV cancer, it's about time to engage with urgency with the question of how to live life. After living as if I was going to die tomorrow or in a few months, maybe it's time for me to rethink my mental model—in fact, I may not be dying very soon. The question about how to really live life matters a great deal, and yet there is confusion around how to answer it. To me, the confusion has simply to do with how the question is contemplated. If someone uses the right methods, the question is answerable without much difficulty. Let's first think of this issue methodically. When someone asks you how they should act regarding a specific condition in order to achieve a certain goal, your mind should be able to grasp that encounter. To begin, think about what constitutes a particular encounter. Take, for example, meetings with your primary care doctors as you work to maintain your health. Now that you've identified the unit (or episode, incident, or instance of something) of what you're trying to comprehend, you can examine the elements that constitute that unit. If we consider life as what we want to examine, for example, the question would be: What is the unit of life? That's the question that needs to be answered before embarking on any further exploration.

The unit of life, the basic building block, or the atom of life (call it what you want) is an experience. An experience is what people tell stories about to someone else who can understand and relate to it. An experience is what a subject lives in time and space, interacting with others, and acting in this way or that. An experience can be examined from the outside, provided we set the scope of what we are describing correctly. And that's it. If you truly grasp this idea, you have already achieved 95 percent of the goal of this book. The rest are details. Note here, I am not only speaking of those high moments that give you joy or meaning, such as the graduation of your child or your marriage. I am speaking of your experiences, regardless of what value you attribute to them.

So now, if someone asks you what life is, the answer becomes easy. The life of a person is the entirety of the experiences that individual has gone through in time between the beginning and end points of their existence. I refer to time here simply as we all commonly experience it, in the form of minutes, hours, days, and years. I'm not much concerned here about an organism's actual start of life, whether it's the first breath or heartbeat, or an incident that happened millions of years ago. Nor do I much care about the medical definition of death or people's views on this. What matters to me essentially is the life experience that the person involved in can understand and communicate to others. It is a simple and straightforward approach.

For those interested in philosophy, sharing how some methods work may be useful. I simply moved the question "What is life?" from ontology and axiology to epistemology. By that, I mean I am no longer interested in the being of life, and I couldn't care less (for the purposes here) about whether we are living a morally good life. I am simply proposing a framework that facilitates people's thinking about real-life issues and finding practical answers to their questions. My approach is about learning and understanding while shaping positions around a particular experience or topic that will guide our subsequent actions.

Thinking about life as experiences opens up infinite possibilities to shape your life toward becoming authentically you. It also opens up possibilities for communities to emerge that can support their members in their pursuit of self-actualization without the constraints of an a priori framework. Indeed, this conceptualization opens up horizons of possibilities. Yet, it also has a supporting structure that allows for and facilitates the working through of the challenge at hand: namely answering the question of how to live. Moreover, it frees you from the bad habit of thinking vaguely and poetically when what is needed is sharp and nuanced thinking. It further protects you from succumbing to religious frameworks that can be dangerous to the authentic self and need to be called out or shunned.

Life as sets of experiences is not the only answer to the question "What is life?" Looking at a few other answers can also be instructive. However, I do not intend to organize these other ideas methodically. I mainly want to focus on contrasting these other positions with my approach. If you ask a hundred people, "What is life?" you'll get 300 answers, even though most people don't bother to ask themselves that question; they just carry on living! The common responses can be grouped into two main categories: 1) life is a legacy that is made up of one's achievements, and 2) life is the set of moral choices that one's actions reflect. There are also more vague and poetic answers, such as, "Life is the breath you take while you're in the moment," "Life is the bonds you form," and "Life is the time you spend doing what's meaningful to you."

These answers can be satisfying at times, especially during a specific phase in life. However, they do not methodically address the fundamental question of what is life and provide an answer at the level I'm interested in. People will readily offer these answers to you, and you may find yourself buying into them. After all, who hasn't pursued achievements and success? But a legacy of this nature is more fitting for a résumé than for answering an existential question. I have yet to hear of someone dying who, in their last moment, asked to take a final look at their undergraduate diploma from Harvard or their PhD from Yale. When one views life as a set of achievements, there is the danger of being stuck in pursuing results rather than simply enjoying the journey and just being oneself. For me, this is a good critique of the life as achievements argument.

RELIGIONS. My nemeses here are not those obsessed with success—I call those people the "simply immature," who will have to take a few falls and pick themselves up before they learn what really matters in life. My true enemies are the religious fanatics who have developed a moral grading system to judge and regulate every single action in life. I'm not speaking here of only the most extreme Muslims, Christians, Jews, Buddhists, or Hindus. Indeed, the moderate ones who have the same mindset are just as bad and, in fact, are even more damaging because they're harder to identify and neutralize. Religions have built entire systems that serve to pass judgment on every action we take, and those judgments become an internalized force that shapes our future behaviors. This force directs a person's succession of actions. Cumulatively, it can ruin a person's whole life, and what a waste this is! Religions condition people to assume the mindset of pupils in a classroom, presenting their homework to merely get praise. It's pathetic, sad, and funny all at the same time. Both individually and collectively, we could do much better with less religion-based moralistic judgments of our day-to-day actions. Remember that religions were created in different times and places. They are the inventions of people who are like you, except they were less evolved morally, psychologically, and cognitively. Today, we can construct a better system for understanding our lives. We have at hand tools that were unavailable a few hundred years ago, let alone a few centuries or millennia ago.

THE NEW AGE FOLKS. A similar enemy of mine are the new age folks, who are all about breathing and being in the moment, shouting, "Breathe! Breathe! Keep breathing!" They annoy me, not just because they trigger my traumas (when I get my lung CT scan every six months, the machine says, "Breathe! Hold your breath! Breathe!") but because they frequently lack nuance and substance. I know that living requires us to breathe. Breathing is powerful, and I use it consciously to regulate my emotions. I also meditate fairly often, using breathing as a focus. However, answering the question of what life is by claiming it's a sequence of breaths or the moments lived is just as meaningless as the air it takes to utter that statement. Time is simple, and a moment is the nearest something can be to the void. To me, time is like a vessel that needs to be filled. I need substance to glut my appetite, and the new age folks have very little of that to feast on.

RELATIONSHIPS. I respect the folks who refer to relationships when talking about life and its meaning. I owe a great deal to those with whom I share kinship—my parents, siblings, friends, and loved ones who have graced me with their lives and experiences. But here is the key. In exploring the question of what life is, some additional nuance is required, and answering this question by referring to relationships lacks most of that nuance. The bonds themselves are not what matters: it's the quality of the experiences created along the way in forming those genuine bonds that is of essential importance.

Examples of experiences

I have sought to construct a conceptual tool that is sufficiently flexible yet allows for concrete examination, and I believe I have found that: Life is a set of experiences. However, in my arguing of that notion, one might understandably ask, "But what's an experience? What is this unit of life you've been talking about?" To answer this question, as a pragmatist, I have set a goal to clarify what I mean when I use the concept "experience." Here, I will refer to the experiences that are familiar to most people. As I do so, you can understand the concept and learn how to use it in similar settings.

1. DRINKING COFFEE. Right now, I'm drinking coffee. In front of me is a ceramic mug, half-filled with the rich, dark liquid. The coffee is warm, and I taste its mildly acidic and slightly bitter flavor. Suppose I asked you about your experience drinking a cup of coffee. You could probably think of five to ten elements that go along with this experience. Then, if I asked you to think about incidents in your life that have shaped your perception of this experience, you could probably easily list a further ten. For example, I might think of drinking my mom's coffee, which was mild in flavor but rich with love. I might also think of one time when I was on my own drinking coffee in Damascus. I was trying to write a poem about jasmine, imagining I was like the poet Nizar Qabani, but nothing came from my efforts. It turns out that Damascus's jasmine does not inspire everyone! Rather than an inspirational teapot, I learned that Damascus is not necessarily a haven for justice or equity. Returning to this time of my life, I ponder on the two cups of coffee I drink every day, one in the morning when I wake up and one in the afternoon after my nap. I seem to need coffee to keep going and enjoy living. I reflect on how my attachment to coffee and my savoring of it has come from these prior experiences, especially from my mom. She loved her coffee in the morning, and I often made it for her and shared her pleasure in drinking it.

2. A WALK WITH THE DOG. It becomes a bit more complex when we consider the experience of doing things with others. Even in moving from drinking a cup of coffee in solitude to taking one's dog on a morning walk, a higher complexity is involved. In considering the experience of walking my dog, I will focus on one occurrence. For example, one Saturday morning I woke up and made my coffee first thing, as usual. While in the kitchen, I fed my dog, Leo, who, after gobbling it up ravenously, lay back down and waited for the big event. That was at about 7:45 a.m. After my music lesson that morning, which ended at 8:30, I put on Leo's collar and leash, and we left my apartment. We took the elevator, and I walked him outside to his favorite tree, right in front of the building. He sniffed to take note of all the dogs that had marked that tree since he last had and proceeded to do his business. We returned to the apartment, where I removed his leash, praised him, and let him roam free. This was an uneventful experience, and for that, I am grateful. He didn't get into a barking match with Cacheo, our neighbor's dog. I didn't have to keep him on a shorter leash while the other dogs walked by. I didn't run into the old White woman who lives next door, the one who once said to me, "I'm okay with your dog in the elevator but not you!" If I reflect on my thoughts and feelings a little more, I realize that I don't really

enjoy walking Leo. He likes it, and he's usually very excited to go outside. In his enthusiasm, he jumps around in anticipation, but my energy doesn't match his at all. I live in a tiny apartment, and he likes to butt my face or eyes with his snout when I bend over to tie my shoelaces getting ready to go out. I dislike these walks, but he loves and looks forward to his little breaks in our dull days. If I ask you about your experience with your pet or child, you will likely describe elements that are different from my experience.

3. DATING.

Our life experience becomes even more complex when we consider our relationships with other human beings. For example, let's look at the experience of going on a date. If I try to describe that experience, I might first say something about a lady I met, for example. She had distinguished green eyes, which she was very proud of because "green eyes are rare." She had white skin, a sharply angled nose, and lips that were neither too full nor too thin. She had obtained two master's degrees, and she bragged about this accomplishment. She walked so fast in the park that I almost had to run after her. She talked about taking time away from "serious dating" to focus on self-care. In fact, she talked about three-quarters of our time together! I thought it would be better to get to know each other as just friends, which I texted her. She did not respond.

4. WRITING A BOOK.

The fourth and last experience I will describe here is quite interesting to me and relevant to what I'm doing at the moment. It's the experience of writing this book. I had the idea of writing about laughter a long time ago, after I'd finished the manuscript about love. Since that time, I had jotted down some thoughts, but I hadn't fully developed the thesis. Now, I am engaged in doing just that. I'm sitting at my computer, staring at the screen on which the words are emerging. My brain is entertaining ideas about this experience of writing. It's a structured process at this stage; I have completed the brainstorming phase and outlined the content. Now I am developing the substance, which I plan to repeatedly revise. I am observing myself as I write. I didn't initially plan to write about the experience of producing a book, but I thought it would help me regarding this part of the work. This strategy occurred to me as I sat down and felt the heaviness of the task of writing. Writing is emotionally and mentally draining. But the struggle is worth it. I am jotting down notes rather than playing music or singing, which are my favorite activities these days. When I think about this experience, I naturally compare it to the experiences of authoring my first three books. I felt miserable at times writing my other books, whereas I am more relaxed with the whole process now.

REFLECTIONS ON THE EXAMPLES. Now that I have presented these four experiences, I want to take time to sit with them in order to comprehend them better. The way I do this is to spend time sensing, perceiving, feeling, and thinking about the key elements of each experience. I could think about them all together and attempt to focus on one element of each that falls in the same category—for example, time. I mentioned that I enjoy drinking my coffee every morning. However, this morning, I had my coffee but didn't finish it; I was too tired for it to even kick in. I checked the clock to see if I had time to take a nap. I paused to think about when I should walk my dog; his last walk was when I had some free time before my regular Saturday family Skype meeting. His walk usually doesn't take more than a few minutes. Also, now that I'm dating, I wondered why I thought about a specific person today. It's been a month since my breakup, and I'm putting myself out there again. I feel that this experience has helped me heal. I realized that the person I loved dearly and the one I couldn't care less about have something in common— they both have little interest in me. Then, while drafting the book, I am again considering the time, thinking about this long holiday weekend and hoping to finish the first draft by the end of the weekend.

Notice that in addition to time, I was thinking about some related elements. I had to extend my thoughts to include these other elements; if not, I would have been simply ticking off the time that I spend on each experience or recounting the exact hour of each occurrence. These numerical "data" are next to meaningless for me regarding my lived experiences. Also, when my mind went to those aspects related to time, I didn't necessarily address the same time-related aspects for all four experiences. I talked about the time of day in the first two experiences, whereas I talked about the broader concept of time concerning healing from a relationship in the last one. Our personal stories can be extremely complex, and we need to be free to organize them within structures that are meaningful to us.

Let's step away from time to my original task of reflecting on what I actually did. If I want to examine a particular experience, I need to be able to name the elements of that experience so that I can sufficiently describe it to someone. I also need to know the kinds of elements involved so that I can intentionally describe the specific categories that are relevant. Aside from the time category, I can think of countless others. For those that are relevant to me, I'll mention my feelings and needs. For example, how did I feel when I drank my coffee, walked my dog, went on a date, and wrote the book? What did I want or expect when I lived these experiences?

Another relevant category is how I relate to these experiences. What are my positions? How am I participating? What is it that I'm doing? What are some of my other related experiences? No less important are those categories related to the elements that constitute the ingredients of the experiences. What is coffee? How do you make it? Who's my dog? Who's the person I went on a date with? What is my book about?

Let's not forget an important class of categories related to the normative and evaluative space I operate within. Following Jurgen Habermas's theory of communicative action, norms and values occupy their own world, the social world in which we determine what's good and acceptable. It's clearly okay to drink coffee, so maybe this doesn't apply so much in that respect. However, with my dog, for example, how do I make sure I am giving him the care he needs? Also, how do I approach my date with respect and authenticity? How do I write a book that's meaningful for me and others? How should I think about this subject? What should my framework be? Are there other, better frameworks I could use to categorize and talk about experiences? This probing is vital because as we think about experiences and learn to appreciate them in order to understand and potentially reshape our lives, we are working with the elements of these categories—both the normative and evaluative.

From describing to modifying

The question that matters most to me in this book, however, is "Can we modify our experience?" Hell, yeah, of course we can; otherwise, why would I be writing this book? We adjust our experiences all the time, often with ease and without even thinking about it.

To set the stage, when I speak of changing an experience, I mean it in the everyday sense. Say that someone is asked to describe an experience of some kind that they are living in the moment, and then they are asked the same question at a different time. They would likely provide different answers at these different times. Let's run through a few examples. Think of your most recent grocery shopping experience. Be mindful of some elements of it, such as where you went for your groceries, the route to the store, and so on. Then, think about how you did your grocery shopping in a different time frame, let's say a few years back or before you moved to your current address. The experiences have shared elements—maybe you've always bought Cheerios, milk, and eggs. But they also have some new elements. For example, maybe you used to shop at Kroger's, but now you buy your groceries online from Amazon (yikes!). From this standpoint, you can see that your experience of grocery shopping has changed. This is what I mean when I talk about changing an experience. The elements of the experience might be like night and day from the first occurrence to the second, even though the experience itself may be labeled the same, that is, "buying groceries."

Let's consider a little more what can be altered in an experience. In thinking of what you can modify in an experience, you may want to first state what you cannot change without the experience becoming completely different. This is what I call "limit-setting modifications." This is where an experience is no longer the same as how it started but has become something else. To return to the previous example about drinking coffee in the morning, you could change the cup you drink it from, the source of the beans, where you drink your coffee, and the time of day you drink it. However, if you drink mint tea instead of coffee, it won't be a coffee drinking experience anymore. Still, you might say, "I made a small change in my life today; I was bored, so during my coffee time, I drank mint tea." In that case, people will understand what you mean. You're referring to an experience that's culturally familiar to others—coffee time—and you can speak about it from the standpoint of a participant in that culture. Furthermore, you can use the reference more or less metaphorically (or you might say "loosely").

Instead of taking the elevator every day when I take my dog for a walk, I could take the stairs. I could also take him to the park nearby, which would be exercise for me, and I could reach my 10,000 steps. Furthermore, I could wake up earlier to avoid the neighbors and other obstacles on our short walk. But if I hire a dog walker, I could probably no longer talk about my experiences walking my dog, even though he would still be going on walks.

Also, I could say, "Man, I'm so tired of this online dating scene. I'm going to focus on activities that I enjoy." As I go out and participate in, for example, hiking groups, I am technically suspending my intention to date and therefore I can no longer speak of dating as a current experience. Now, even though I'm genuinely only looking to find friends, who knows, maybe someday a connection could evolve into an intimate one. But let's say I happen to find a friend and we start spending exclusive time getting to know one another and exploring being intimate. Now, once again, I can talk about the experience of dating in the here and now.

Finally, I could modify how I write. Instead of seeking quiet and solitude in which to write, sitting in the dark typing my way through this manuscript, I could find a community of writers. I would still keep many elements of the experience, such as the topic and using a computer. I could use a pen to write the manuscript.

In the above examples, I have described modified elements of the experiences. I intentionally 'flipped' an idea into something else. I added or subtracted a position by using Habermas's concept of "validity claim," which relates to what a person verbally expresses about the positions they hold on the aspects emerging in their worlds. Validity claims are relevant to three worlds, according to Habermas. The first is the world of the subject (statements about what I want, wish, desire, or need). This is called the subjective world, which I, and only I, have privileged access to. The second is the world of objects (statements about what exists around us and the relationships between them that explain how the world we observe and access works). Finally, there is the social world (statements that affirm or negate the normative and evaluative positions of the subject). This is our shared social world, in which our normative reasoning, value judgments, and aesthetic perceptions are interconnected.

It works like this. I twist an element in the experience by changing a claim I am making as part of taking a position. I then find other supportive claims to ground the new one and adjust the contradictory ones in my mind to stay consistent. In my actions, I make sure I am following my stated claims. In a nutshell, that is how I change my experiences.

Let's go back to the coffee drinking example. Instead of taking the position "I'm drinking black coffee," I can change it to "I'm drinking my coffee with sugar and milk." I simply add sugar and milk to be entitled to this new claim. At that moment, the experience is different. I can also choose to remember my mom, so I look at her photo while drinking coffee and feel the warmth of her presence, about which I can then say a few words. If I choose to take longer walks with my dog, I remind myself that it's my responsibility to also take care of my health by exercising. I want to live as long as possible. Exercising is a means of reaching that goal, and longer walks are a step in that direction. In the process of taking different positions and making different claims, I am bringing elements that were not salient before to the same experience. Perhaps I let go of my desperation to find a mate online and instead resolve to experience and enjoy the world more fully, whether single or in a relationship. In doing so, I take the stance that life is about the experience, and I shouldn't wait to find that one special person to share it with. I will instead share it with the people who offer their care and support, such as my close friendships. Finally, when I choose to write with others,

I am affirming that if I connect with a community of authors, I may be the catalyst for someone else's true expression, perhaps even their masterpiece. By sharing with others in this way, I might even enjoy the writing process more. We should support one another in this wild world of writing. It's not a competition; interacting with others around creative expression can be fun!

To sum up, we defined what an experience is while looking at a few examples. Then, we examined what it means to modify the elements of that experience, and we sketched a conceptual model for thinking about these elements. Now that we have this model and can recognize our capacity to effectively modify our experiences, we are ready to live life! But that takes practice.

Practice, practice, and practice more!

Practice makes all the difference. I know this statement pisses off people who are obsessed with genetic susceptibilities and individual talents and abilities. I don't buy the argument that it's all in our genes and we are born with natural gifts. Those who believe this often cling to this mental model to explain their "failures" to themselves! Fuck them. They can believe whatever they want, but I insist it's all about practice. We learn by doing, and when we reach a certain skill level through dedicated practice, we have the chance to exercise our capacity to develop mastery. Mastery is nothing but an exercised—thus cultivated—ability to do something well. Yes, I know, not everyone who practices basketball will be a Michael Jordan. Although I am unlikely to become the next Habermas or Hegel, still I will aim to achieve my full potential and actualize myself through practice. I will learn, and I will learn how to learn. What other options are there? I don't want to remain the person I am right now, staying stuck in life like many people unfortunately are.

But how do we learn and practice making changes in our lives? To answer this, I will first summarize what we've just discussed. We have looked at sets of exercises that increase in complexity. We started by recognizing what an experience is. We then considered a few simple and common experiences. After that, we broke those experiences down into their core elements. We spent time appreciating these various elements, including organizing them into categories. We were then ready to contemplate how these elements can change within an experience and how these modifications can entirely alter the experience. We did this intentionally, using language to define what constitutes a change, and we developed a conceptual framework for the change itself.

Now, here we are, ready to practice until we become fluent in the steps outlined above. There aren't that many steps, really. Lentil soup is made with more than five steps. You don't believe me? Think about the last time you made lentil soup. Better yet, here is a Syrian recipe: You buy the ingredients from a store or get them delivered. They are onions, lentils, pita bread, and olive oil. I love to add garlic—who doesn't love garlic? You chop the onion and add it to a bowl of lentils. Then, you add water at a ratio of three or four to one, depending on how thick you want your soup. You can vary the elements of this experience of making lentil soup by adding potatoes instead of sauteed pita bread. The key is to add them early so they soften and dissolve. In the end, you need that balance between protein and carbs. That's why pita bread is excellent. So there you have it; making lentil soup is an experience with elements you can modify. If you've never made lentil soup, now you have learned how, and that's a bonus you didn't expect from this book on laughter, did you?

What I've tried to show is that you can think of your life as a set of experiences, and you can modify the elements of each experience. In other words, you can choose how you encounter what takes place in your life. You have the freedom to make choices. This straightforward notion is the essence of liberation. When I think of this kind of liberation, my heart beats faster with anxiety and, dare I say it, fear. This idea is simple enough, but it will push you out of your comfort zone. True, it's within your power to modify the elements of your lived experience. But that is not to say it's always easy. My goal here is to help you develop the mastery you need to reform your lived experiences. Once you develop the mastery to change, then what was hard becomes more easily accessible, and with practice it can be done well. That's the definition of mastery, executing skills without facing much of a challenge. So let's keep practicing!

Slow your excited heart and don't panic. I care about your well-being, and I won't throw you off a cliff. My goal is not to disrupt your life just for the fun of it. We'll move forward slowly, and we'll laugh along the way.

Changing experiences toward something

Now that we've seen that experiences can be altered by one's actions and choices, a question naturally arises. Can someone intentionally reform their experiences in a specific direction? We frequently hear people speak about being positive as a desirable attitude. We also hear about adopting gratitude as a preferred response to life events or interactions with others. We are also familiar with people bracketing, which means suspending engagement with an idea for the time being, or avoiding, which means not dealing with the subject but rather pushing it away from the conscious mind. All these choices alter how one lives or perceives an experience. I am describing these general choices that people can make to keep salient the idea that, yes, we do indeed reform our experiences all the time.

The strategy is not highly complex. To be positive, it is suggested to look at the glass as half full instead of half empty. Here, there is an experience— literally or figuratively—with a glass of liquid. The element that you can choose to keep salient in your mind is how much of the liquid you have left instead of how much is gone. You keep that awareness within the experience so that you can do certain things with it, such as drinking with joy and less worry, instead of being anxious about running out of the liquid. So, taking this analogy further, to learn to be more positive, you break an experience into elements. When thinking about the elements, you choose the language that describes the aspects of the experience that are more uplifting, open, happy, and accepting rather than the opposite aspects. You select a schema or framework that constitutes a more optimistic view and leave behind those elements that produce a darker feeling, thought, or attitude.

I have never been that kind of "positive person." In fact, I'm annoyed by the "try to be positive" people. I call a positive fanatic who only sees things through rosy lenses a "Posy Rosy." For this person, it's all good, all the time. Posy Rosies are annoying even when they're on their own and not bothering anyone. But all too often, they get in your face with their "Be positive!" messages. At times, I just want them to fuck off and go to hell to drink their half-full glass there.

Then, you've got the gratitude people. If I want to be grateful, I simply infuse my lived experiences with statements such as, "I am grateful for this or that." This position can be supported by a normative stance that "I am not entitled to what I'm given. But now that I have it, I feel lucky as a recipient of an act of grace that I don't necessarily deserve." This attitude also brings in a simple view about reality—shit happens! If we have a day with no shit, let's celebrate! But it becomes a little too much when people push their gratitude to the extreme. I call these folks the "Grat Frats." They spout, "You should be grateful" when you're miserable. It just so happens that they are often the whiniest when things are not going well for them. But even if they're consistent with their advice, I don't care much for these people, either; just shut up and let me whine! Many of them live in near perfect worlds because of their unearned privilege. Yet they want everyone else, including those who have very little, to say thank you continually.

I intentionally mixed the avoidant and bracketing groups together. I think we all do one or the other to some extent, depending on our bandwidth and capacities. When I am overwhelmed, I wish I could just avoid certain things and simply stick my head in the sand. Luckily, I don't need to do that very often. I am lucky. I've developed sophisticated coping skills that allow me to bracket distressing subjects and put them to the side until I have the bandwidth to deal with them. In both cases, however, my engagement with the experience I encounter is altered by my choice to participate now or hold off on participating.

Without further ado, let me put my cards on the table. I think you're ready to accept the two main hypotheses of this book: we can laugh at almost any life experience if we choose to, and we can let go of the elements of nearly every life experience if we want to. That's really the gist of the book. I'm convinced that laughing and letting go are such powerful positions, attitudes, strategies, or, dare I say, answers to our existential questions, that we need to learn and practice them, and we need to do that today. Delaying learning how to laugh and let go means experiencing a loss that can be avoided and a suffering that can be prevented. It also means that beautiful experiences that could have been lived are lost. By laughing and letting go, you're not sacrificing your authenticity and lying to yourself to live. You don't have to give up your stubborn humanness to accept that what's given to you is okay. Because guess what? You can be grateful as much as you want, but the situation is often not okay. If you're not happy about it, why the fuck are you grateful? You're often mistreated and not allowed the choices that are available to others. You're oppressed, and your life can be hell, but on top of that, you need to say thank you or focus on the positive by lying to yourself? That is the definition of misery. I'm sorry, but I do not want to participate in that.

Conversely, you can be free, but not in the sense of not suffering in this life. No one has guaranteed that life will be a pleasant walk in the park. But you can be free in the sense of laughing at it and letting go of whatever has a hold on you. That piece of shit who made you mad is not worthy of your anger. You recognize them as worthy when you engage with them in anger or frustration. Laugh at their assholeness and at how you let them make you feel. As another example, if the person who gave you love and care even though you didn't deserve it chose to move on without you, simply say thank you and carry on with your life. It was a good time while it lasted! Laugh at your silliness, let go, and forget about them. Your ex-lover will be way happier without you. You might be way happier, too; trust me on this. Just think of some of the sleepless nights you have had over them. You were missing out on other good things in life.

What do you think is *so important* for you to attain? Is it really that important? Or did you *make* it that important? Or worse, did someone else fuck you up and make it that important for you? Let go and laugh as you discover this truth today. Do it before it's too late! You're still alive, and you can do something with your life rather than remain that proverbial hamster on the wheel. However, more important than this liberation of what holds you back is that when you laugh and let go, you'll be in a place to do something good. You will be able to choose your experiences and how you will live them. You will be able to name your life project and work on it. You will be able to author your story. Are you ready to laugh and let go? I sure as hell am.

Laughing

I fell in love with a woman who captured my whole heart. I can still paint the moments in my imagination when I first saw her and replay our conversations. I fell in love right away, with the first kiss. But my love for her grew faster than hers for me, and our relationship went down a bumpy road. I got into therapy to help me manage my emotions and to understand and accept her perspective. I've done extensive self-development work to learn how to approach relationships with respect for my partner as an equal and to love and care for her. I wanted a woman's point of view to make sure I was being consistent with my thoughts and feelings. A woman therapist, I thought, would be a helpful sounding board, and she was, even though my love relationship did not work out. The remote online sessions worked well for a while.

When my love affair ended, I went back to dating. I quickly recognized that I felt challenged in approaching White women, and I shared this difficulty with my White woman therapist. I explained to her that I could not ascertain if the person I am with (1) is being authentic and caring, (2) has grown out of their prejudices, (3) is somewhat racist and keeping that part hidden away, or 4) is a full-blown racist. It's easy for me to call out the latter to someone's face. I've had enough experiences with White women of each of these four types to support the validity of this typology.

The therapist recognized my concern and recommended the book *Totality and Infinity*. According to the book's author, Emmanuel Levinas, she explained, it is an act of violence to make a totalizing claim about any person. I was taken aback by her remark. I could understand that she was attempting to relate to my interest in philosophy by sharing this particular book. I could also see how she was offering support by providing me with a concept/tool that could add nuance to the issue, recognizing the conflict I was experiencing around it. I never want to put any person in a box. Yet, the more I mulled over that conversation, the more uncomfortable I felt. I sat on my couch and stared at the computer screen for a while not knowing what to say.

I felt triggered. While my therapist was finishing her master's degree, taking a "full course on Levinas," I was back home in Syria, struggling my way through school with little mentoring or support. I was witnessing violence perpetrated on the people I loved. I also was the victim of physical violence and witnessed my best friends beaten by the secret police. After four months of living in the liberal city of Madison, Wisconsin, I was deemed incompetent by a supervising attending physician (a White woman), who had spent little time with me, and, as a result, I lost my job. Similarly, when I went into the dating world in the diverse city of Orlando, Florida, I met someone who said, "You Arabs/terrorists, why did you do 9/11?" After that, I lived in Indiana, where I often felt like the unseen immigrant, receiving looks of doubt about whether I was a risk. I have encountered violence aimed at me from both the right and left. I have been perceived and treated by White women as less trustworthy or dangerous and by some as their "Middle Eastern male fetish." Now, with my therapist, here I was again, the subject of a White woman's skewed perceptions. I shared with her my struggles around dating White women, and she chose to focus on the interpretation of my experience as somehow my committing violence! My unspoken thought in reflecting on this was, "Gosh! This is so typical!"

I spent a whole week thinking about that interaction and unpacking it until I remembered what a Black woman who was a mentor to me once said: "You struggle and spend your days and nights thinking, reflecting, and making sense of the other person's position. Yet, the other person probably doesn't even notice or care about the whole incident. You monitor your actions and apologize when you feel you have stepped over the line. But no one apologizes to you."

This time, I decided to deal with the situation differently and to end my therapy. I am done trying to make sense of the other person's position in situations like this. I am done trying to carry the burden of understanding the nuances of the situation alone. I am tired, period! I now choose to totalize however I want and commit the violence of laughing! I reassure myself that laughing does not negate the work that can and needs to be done to unpack a conflict or struggle. I can still endeavor to understand the "good intentions" of my therapist. I can also do the work of reconstructing her position in all its complexity and nuances. I know I am capable of doing this, but it will take a lot of effort, and I have other things I want to do with my life. I simply cannot afford to do all that work with every interaction I have, even though I still need to do it periodically in many contexts. But what I need most is laughter, which provides a shortcut to the resolution of complex matters so that I can move on, at least for the time being.

By uttering a phrase with humorous intentions, I commit the violence of bringing together complex issues in one or two words. The violence lies precisely in reducing the other person to their attributes, exaggerating the aspects of the matter, overlooking other factors, neglecting certain sides of an issue, and handling ideas with little nuance. Yes, you heard me correctly— with little nuance. The good thing is that this violence is acceptable because I am inflicting it with humor and laughter. Listeners know they're missing a lot of the details from me; they know the joker always omits some information. But that's precisely why it's humor. When presenting a story to amuse oneself or the other for the sake of laughter, you don't need all the details. Remember the last time someone explained a joke? Was it funny after the unpacking? Yeah, probably not. When communicating from an attitude of humor, you're not supposed to have all the details. What's more, the fact that you're allowing yourself to commit this violence is an essential part of being funny.

Think of a cartoon or sketch. You replace a person with a few lines. You don't bother to paint shades of color to give the impression they are three-dimensional figures. Who cares? It's a cartoon! It's not Michelangelo's *Last Judgment*.

You will indeed need some details to set the stage and talk about the context. But just as you don't get your news from a comedian making jokes onstage, others won't judge you for missing details if you make them laugh! The comedian who writes sketches blurs the details and, in doing so, gives their story a sense of timelessness. Often, they take the specifics out of a certain context so that they can be applied to other contexts. The details are only relevant if they support the punch line. Ask yourself what the punch line is. Note that it's called the "punch line" because it's supposed to have a strong effect—enough to make people laugh, indeed sometimes shock them into laughter. Thus, laughing is violent, and that's okay!

We laugh to heal

When we experience a situation and it grips our minds, we get stuck in one flavor of affect/feeling. If we're feeling gloomy, we see the world through the darker-tinted colors. In turn, that depressing mood will cause us to latch onto events that confirm our state. It's like a mental schema or framework; it searches for what fits and avoids any evidence that doesn't.

When we are severely attacked, we may participate in violence. By reacting with violence, we violate our own principles and are therefore inconsistent with how we would like ourselves to be. This inconsistency causes us pain. It takes psychological work to come to a position that resolves these paradoxes. It takes effort to harmonize our thoughts. This task can be daunting, and often people give up and, by default, continue to live in misery. But when you approach your experiences with humor, you can do away with the need to reconcile these positions. You can accept things as not fitting and take them as they are. In fact, you seek precisely what doesn't fit. The discomfort you are feeling, if related to within a space of humor, will instead become a source of amusement.

I am fed up with racist people who spend their time in so-called "anti-bias" training workshops so that they can manage their racism and how they express it. All they hear is, "You do this. You do not do that." It's mostly about how they present themselves outwardly, and, therefore, more like public relations work rather than trying to be a better person.

Lazy-ass racists don't usually go into psychotherapy to discover how their heads got messed up to believe they are superior to others. Instead, they continue harming others by the way they roll their eyes, purse their lips, and let thoughtless and insensitive shit slip out of their mouths. It takes months and years of therapy to figure out how mom or dad made little Jonny feel that led him to acting this way. And now big racist-ass Jonny is making everyone else who is different from him miserable. It angers me that people of color and immigrants like me are the ones who end up needing therapy to manage the trauma and pain inflicted by unhinged Jonnies.

Then, you get a therapist telling you to be open to the person and not assume motives.

God, just take my life now!

As an immigrant, people look at me as someone who should be grateful until the end of my life because I got accepted to this country. By whom? By people whose ancestors stole the land after wiping out the original owners? To that, I say, fuck your ancestors, and fuck you, too! Okay, now that I have released some tension, I will take a moment to laugh and then get back to work.

Laughter keeps me sane and helps me fight back by saying no to the nonsense. There is a level of complexity that I could engage in to unpack and understand others' positions. But I do not want to engage in that now. I'll release the tension by wrapping the subject in humor. I don't always have the bandwidth to empathize.

Humor helps me and others who have had to navigate through life from a place of little power. There are many powerful people who are inauthentic. They speak adamantly about the need for authenticity and care, but they never mean what they say. Their actions belie their words. They take themselves very seriously and lack any sense of humor. With these people, I use humor as well. I can neutralize their harmful effects on my soul by calling them names as I learn to set my own boundaries. They are like snakes that will squeeze the soul out of you at every opportunity, all the while filling your ears with talk about their generosity that is cloaked in venom. I protect myself by calling them rattle-tailed snakes, shitheads, or other sweet words of this kind!

Humor is violence, yes. Humor is totalizing, true. But it's also vitally needed to survive. At the same time, it doesn't deny the infinite nature of everyone or the possibility that things are not always or only as they seem. This is precisely what I am attempting to communicate. Humor is totalizing in a nuanced way. It's coming up with an image or metaphor that makes sense of the experience by showing an odd aspect that's hidden or unseen. People do not usually talk about this aspect because they are afraid of it and cannot find the language to put it into words. We, however, can develop the sensitivity to identify and capture such elements and explore the unspoken nuances. Resistance through humor is quite sophisticated. And the most sophisticated way is, in fact, the simplest. Remember, you can laugh at the person who has done terrible things; it's perfectly okay.

We laugh to love

Laughter is not only used to fight, defend, and protect ourselves; we also laugh to connect with those we love. If you want to feel loved and receive joy, spend time with a laughing six-month-old infant. If you attempt to put into words your experience of what they're trying to say, it sounds like this:

The infant says, "Hey, I'm here. You're really interesting and big, but I feel safe with you. See me. I see that you see me, and that makes me very happy. I'm cute, and I think you know that I'm cute. In fact, I think I'm too cute for you to take your eyes off of me. And if you think I'm funny looking with my big head and small body, that's okay; you were there once, too. You, too, look unusual to me; you've got big ears and a big nose. But don't feel bad; you just look funny."

Meanwhile, you're over there thinking, "This baby is so adorable! What should I do to make them happy so they keep looking at me? My oxytocin level is through the roof right now. Look at this harmless little infant; they'd never hurt me, maybe with their gas, but not with that laugh. Boy, I'm really feeling loved today. I feel special. I made the baby laugh! Yes! I'm such a cool person."

This is what happens when we laugh with someone else. It's peaceful, calm, light-hearted, trusting, safe, connected, caring, giving and receiving, and joy. It's not that much different than you are with a dear friend, lover, or family member who welcomes you with laughter. There is something unconditional about laughing with someone you've just connected with. It's a powerful sign of acceptance. If they laugh along with you, even at a trivial joke or spontaneously with no joke, you know you're in for a good time.

We laugh because we love. It's a choice to laugh. We could choose to put a frown on our faces and present ourselves to the world with tears of woe. Depression is a real condition; for this, I say, get help, period. If you're stuck thinking that you've tried everything but nothing helps, that's because you may be clinically depressed. Again, get help! At times, we laugh for the sake of others. Even though we don't feel like it, we push ourselves to laugh. We prioritize the happiness of the other person and give them a sense of reassurance; this is what I call *love* in my book *A Love Attempt*. Laughter is an effective way of communicating that we're okay. If we're not okay, we can't laugh. By laughing, we're saying that we've got this handled; we have the bandwidth to laugh. If I can't laugh, it means that I have very little capacity to be who I want to be and who others want me to be. You communicate caring to others when you laugh.

We also laugh to attract another person's attention and, maybe, their love. We want to be seen and recognized. The infant wants to be seen, so they develop a social smile to attract attention. Infants are cute anyway, but when they laugh, your heart can't help but feel a connection. Try to tear yourself away from an infant's gaze when they are laughing. You can't; it's like there's some magnet at work! When you laugh on a date, that's a way of showing the other person that you see them and that you want to make them laugh, too. You're telegraphing a promise that you'll be someone who cares about their joy.

Of course, we often laugh judiciously with strangers or randos. It's understandable that people may not respond with random smiles, let alone initiate what might lead to laughter on the metro. A smile can be misinterpreted as an invitation for a conversation when a connection is not desired. Worse, it can be an invitation to a creep, giving them the green light, in their heads, to be even creepier. If a man on the metro sees a woman as a mere sex object, he could perceive a smile as a yes to his unspoken question, "Can I approach?" That's why many people tend not to laugh, smile, or even look strangers in the eye. If they do, they have to find a way to preemptively assert that their boundaries are sealed and that their smile was not an invitation. For example, they may qualify the smile's positive effect with an expression that communicates "but I am not interested."

Because laughter is at the essence of genuine human connectedness, often coming only when our guard is down, some people ("sociopaths"?) employ it manipulatively to get what they want at the expense of others. But that's not very difficult to spot. Laughter is an expression of authenticity. We judge authenticity by the consistency of the action that follows. People who laugh with you to get you to drop your guard, only to influence you externally to get what they want, can be easily called out. I don't worry about it. It also takes extensive training to put on a show of fake laughing. Trust me, you're probably not going to be hurt by someone who laughs.

Don't be afraid to laugh and reciprocate laughter. When you laugh and make others laugh, you give people exactly what they want. Ask a million people what they want, and they will agree that they want to laugh. Just read the posts on dating apps: "I'm looking for someone who makes me laugh!" "I love to laugh!" The desire to laugh, especially with others, is universal. Expressing this desire used to bother the heck out of me. "I'm not your monkey or clown! Why don't *you* make *me* laugh?" I'd swipe left when I saw that on Tinder; I was grouchy as hell. On the downside, I often found myself with grumpy people who didn't know they needed to laugh. God, some dates were pure reciprocal misery! But I laugh at those times now.

The bottom line is that we bond through laughter. Community is not only formed through struggle but also in connection with people with whom we've shared good times. And good times inevitably involve laughter. Those among us who love to care for others might benefit from learning to let go of the need to constantly care for other people. We can also meet people not in their place of misery, but in their space of joy. Maybe if we make them laugh or laugh with them, they wouldn't be so miserable and in need of so much help from doctors or therapists. When I talk to people, I realize that the happier ones know this: we all want to laugh and love laughter. I'm late to the game. But I'm here. I want to laugh, too.

We laugh to not cry

I talked about laughing as a form of resistance when one is triggered and angered by others. I also spoke about laughing to feel the connectedness and warmth of loving. There's also what I consider the third important space for laughter: that space of failed hopes and desires, the one leading to sadness. This is the hardest space of all in which to invite laughter. It may seem that laughing is antithetical to the disappointment experienced when a person's hopes or desires are not fulfilled. Someone who laughs when they lose a loved one, don't get the desired job, or fail an important exam may cause others to worry that they've dissociated from their emotions.

We may not be ready to fully deal with this subject matter at this point of the book. But by the end, I hope you'll have found that in learning to laugh after failed expectations, there is an abundance of meaningful and authentic expressions. However, it takes some work. In this process, letting go is the main element, which will be discussed further in the next chapter. Here, I'll draw only broad sketches.

I would say it is valid to consider it crazy to laugh when your expectations are unmet, but why not? It's perfectly okay to be crazy at times. We live in a crazy world, and maybe letting your craziness out isn't such a bad thing. A rationality framework that evaluatively sets out what's reasonable and unreasonable in people's actions is useful. And it's already there in society, associating a judgment of some sort or the other with every act before we consent. But societal rules aren't set in stone. You can try to write them as commandments on a stone and come up, like Moses, with ten. But really? How can you limit them to a number? Why would you try to fix the fluidity of a social matter? That's mere nonsense. All commandments and religions are nonsense, as I see it.

Really, you can do whatever the fuck you want and react in whatever way you please when you're sad. They might call you crazy, but fuck them! If when you've lost something or someone dear and meaningful to you, you laugh and people tell you to stop it, just give them the middle finger. You do whatever you want and need to heal. You're the miserable one. Those people who come to judge you and dole out advice don't care about you, and you shouldn't care about them, either.

Plus, there are always some funny elements in the experience of dealing with failed expectations or hopes. Even at a funeral, someone might say something silly that makes you laugh. I was devastated when my mom passed away after a car accident. I didn't have the language to deal with her death at that time. My sister was sobbing, and I was crying, too. With far lesser struggles or losses that I'd encountered in my life before mom's death, I'd said things like "Don't worry; it's not a big deal!" But I didn't have anything to say that was helpful in dealing with her death. So I uttered my usual inane statement to my sister, who gave me a look that said, "What do you mean, don't worry; it's not a big deal? Our mom is dead!" I didn't know how to respond or explain. It was an awkward few minutes of me mumbling and trying to pull my foot out of my mouth. I remember that now and laugh.

Since then, this same sister has also passed away. I still can't think of anything to laugh at related to the experience of her death. But I'm a stage IV lung cancer patient myself. Gosh, how frightened of death I am. It's ridiculous, stupid, and funny! I laugh at how death scares the shit out of me. What's there? What's going to happen to me? Yeah, okay, I'll be joining my beloved mom and sister. But hell no, I don't want to join them! Can I just stay here, hanging out with my dad and other siblings? They're good people, too! I think I'm okay with just being here.

Funny true story: whenever my fear of death creeps up on me, I see my sister in my dreams. Since you're everyone in your dreams, I came to believe my sister is my projection. I'd ask me/her if she was afraid of death before dying. I/she would answer, "I was afraid until 9 o'clock. Then I no longer was!" That answer felt good. I now set a timer for the allotted time of the day I am allowed to fear death. When the alarm goes off at 9:00 p.m., time is up, and no more fear!

Elements of a failed relationship can also be funny if you look at them differently. Just think of the obsession you feel with someone who comes into your life. Guess what? This passion you're exuding could be precisely the same for someone with all the same attributes as the lover who just ditched you. Sure, you speak of love, but love comes and goes; think of your high school or college sweetheart. Imagine going back and pining for their love! It's funny what people do for love, and it's also utterly beautiful. Keep doing it. But you should laugh along the way as your heart is squeezed dry like a lemon before moving on in search for another chance to be heartbroken.

In considering easier subjects, similar elements can be found when the outcome of your experience isn't as you desire. For example, I failed a pathology class in medical school. The exam was horrific. I looked at the slides, and all I saw were shades of purple and blue, and they weren't even pretty. I love those colors when they're in the sky at sunset, but on the pathology slides, they felt like an endless Rorschach test I had to repeat over and over. I got two and a half slides correct out of ten, a humiliatingly bad score.

That year was when I hit rock bottom in my academic performance. I was a student activist in medical school, and we protested for democratic reform in Syria. As you can imagine, activism wasn't a walk in the park; in fact, it was extremely stressful. Then, I fell in love with a beautiful Syrian woman who opened my soul to worlds I didn't know existed. We'd spend hours and hours together as she pacified my fears and frustrations with her affection. I remember I was with her the day before my exam. No, I wasn't burning the midnight oil; I was having a good time. Guess what? When you have fun instead of studying before a test, you get your ass handed to you on a silver platter. I had only myself to blame, and I laugh at it now.

Not getting a job or losing a position is no different, so, yes, you can laugh at your disappointments. You heal when you laugh. When you laugh, you demonstrate that you can grow from these experiences. You've already grown when you are able to separate yourself from your disappointments and what made you sad. You see them as part of your many varied experiences along the way. But *you* are still here, and you can keep what you want, bundle it up, and take it with you for the rest of the journey. You can preserve the memories for sure, along with some good laughs.

Whether you're angry, loving, or sad, you've laughed before at different times and on different occasions. And yes, on other occasions, you didn't think something was funny or laughable, but in reality, you could have laughed instead. I would say you were being a bit too serious. I want to think that it's within my capacity to choose when I laugh and when I don't laugh. I don't laugh on command. But I laugh when I allow myself to. I want to let myself laugh and to laugh more. I choose to laugh and be intentional about including more laughter in my life.

I now decide to do this; it's my choice alone. No one will dare say, "No, you cannot do that!" Of course, I can. I literally laughed more drafting this manuscript than I did all of last year combined. And no, I did not all of a sudden become funny. I am who I am. I am just laughing more, whether by myself or with other people. I will also be looking for more opportunities to laugh. I will be searching for what makes me laugh. I will be reminding myself to laugh. I will be sharing my laughter with others. My decision is absolutely to live to laugh. I am proposing this position as an existential answer, and in what follows, you will see why that matters.

Living to laugh is an existential decision

I live to laugh, and that's my choice. I know it's a big claim to make. How can I ground an unusual position like this one? I could try to show that not much else can better fill in the blank in the statement of "I live to . . . ." But that's a difficult one. People might say, "you're a doctor (and doctors save lives!), so why not put, "I live to save lives?" in that blank statement." That's a good thing, too, and I agree. If you can save a life, you totally should. It should never become like, "Ho hum, just another life!" Although it might start to feel that way for people who make a career out of regularly saving lives, it's honorable work. You can also be one more person to add to the herd of people who save lives, and that's great. But that's only one choice among many you can do with your time. You could also work at saving lives at certain times and days and do something else for the rest of the time. No one needs to be saving lives every minute. We're all just human, after all.

Like saving lives, there is honor in lightening someone else's burden of living by laughing with them or making space for them to laugh. Laughter is shared joy. Everyone wants it and responds to it. You're doing something for others when you laugh.

I laugh because it is joy. It's my joy, and I want to have it. It's good that I can potentially share it with others. I appreciate it when someone experiences joy and expresses that emotion with laughter, connecting it with others. In that sense, it can be a shared joy. When I experience joy, I deliberately reach out and connect with others. I seek to lighten the burden I place on others; people don't worry about me when I'm happy. When I allow myself to fall into depression, I am not carrying my own weight. Here I am, back to considering what is my existential answer for others. That's okay, as the self and nonself are quite intertwined. I am not a monad. But it's okay to live like a monad if the person finds joy in it and does not hurt other monads.

I think I can be a person who lives to laugh. I am okay with this. But will others be fine with it? Can living to laugh withstand the critique of others? Let's say I walk into Dante's *Inferno* to meet his friends. Here I find all the philosophers and wise people who have ever contemplated the essence and meaning of life. I hear them saying that we live to love, to know, to connect, to care, to accomplish this or that mission, or to find ourselves. When I say, "I live to laugh," I can hear them chuckling. I don't know if my arguments will be convincing, and I'm nervous! I can see myself in an awkward position, sweating and turning red, and not only from the heat in hell. They are laughing at me! But then, maybe, I start laughing at myself, chuckling right along with them. I set the stage, so, on some level, I knew they would be laughing. I invited and elicited their laughter. I invited it, so it's what I wanted, and that's a success. Maybe I'll be grateful they laughed with me and made me laugh!

However, between now and the time of this meeting in the *Inferno*, I think I can come up with ten good reasons why the statement is valid: (1) Laughing is easy; therefore, I can satisfy the condition that it's doable. I just did it, and people do it right and left. (2) Laughing is available to everyone. I don't have or need to try to have a unique privilege. With that, I satisfy the condition of equitability. Also, people can do it as infants and might even remember how to do it as adults. (3) I can do it with others, but I don't have to have others to participate. I can do it alone. (4) Laughter is empowering and liberating, and even more so when I practice it by myself.

What's more, (5) it brings joy to me and others; thus, it's good. What gives pleasure is good (most of the time). Again, (6) people want it; everyone wants to laugh. Therefore, I can say that it's a desirable action. (7) Not being able to laugh can make a person mean or miserable. Thus, I argue that less laughter isn't desirable. (8) Laughter reduces my pain and the pain of others. It helps us live with less anguish. It helps me and others heal. (9) It brings me to people and other people to me. It allows for the forming of community. Plus, (10) by laughing, people feel a sense of safety through reciprocation. Laughter is connectedness. It's essentially a truthful expression of what one feels that comes from the whole self.

I could go on and on describing how laughter is good; useful; meaningful; desired by everyone; the more of it the better, the less the worse; it's authentic; and it's much, much more. But is that good enough to make the case that "I live to laugh" is a valid position? I'm not sure. How does living to laugh stand up next to leaving a tangible impact on others' lives? Well, if you know a way to make that impact, by all means, go for it. How about living to learn and be enlightened? Isn't that better than living to laugh? Of course, you can live to learn as much as you want. As for me, I live to laugh.

The challenge in grounding this claim is instructive. The past few pages have been my humble attempt at bringing reason to support an existential claim about what someone lives for. Did I succeed?

I don't know! How can we know if I succeeded? Let me try to explain how. You take my position and state your arguments for what fills in the blank in "I live to. . . ." as if I, and other rational beings, are the judges of your reasoning. I would expect you to list the ideas that link the notion you're interested in with what is perceived as good, helpful, meaningful, and authentic. As you can imagine, this set of constructs (e.g., good, helpful, etc.) are what came to mind as representatives of value-laden notions. The sets of constructs for value are not limited to these few items. You can add to them as much as you and the people In your circle want. Two things that come to mind that don't require much grounding in other values are art and music. You can ask an artist who lives to make art why they think it's valid to say, "I live for art!" They'll share a few reasons of the kind that I mentioned: it's enjoyable, healing, beautiful, and so forth. But then, they might add, "But most importantly, I simply do art, and art is something you can devote your whole life to doing." When you hear that from the artist, you're convinced. You don't ask a follow-up question unless you want a piece of art to hit you on your less-sophisticated head!

Let's say someone says something completely unusual and idiosyncratic, like "I live to enjoy the beauty of rocks." I have a friend like that. You might be a little surprised by that statement, but you would still be okay with it. So let me push it further. The person says, "I live to look at rocks." That's a little more interesting, but you can still sort of understand it. If they continue elaborating on this, then, when you reach the point where you don't quite get the meaning and cannot see their perspective, you might say something like, "Well, you do you, boo!" This is the point I want to make here. Honestly, you need to realize that people don't care what you're living your life for and what you consider essential. In today's culture and in the circles of reasonable people, if you say, "I live for (fill in the blank however you want)," the least enthusiastic answer you'll get is, "That's quite interesting!"

You really can do whatever the fuck you want with your life.

I am arguing for living life within a framework that recognizes the experiences that constitute life. Choose whatever you want to prioritize as an element in your lived experiences and live by it. I have attempted to make the case that I have chosen to be content with answering the big existential question in terms of laughter. I am okay with that. I also accept similar answers from others who choose to live life the way they want and for whatever reason they want.

I had a strategic intent in carrying out this exercise. I wanted to challenge myself and others to develop frameworks that offer answers to the question of what one lives for. I am fully aware of the good purposes in life. Justice is, for me, the highest purpose. But there is also prosperity, success, wealth, fame, and others. If you asked me what a life project is that could be worthy of a desired 50 more years of life, my answer would be one in which the person works to bring us closer to social justice. But when I speak about laughing, I am approaching the subject from a different angle. It's another framework. It's not about the goal as an end result; rather, it's about the experiences along the way. This is not a contradiction, but I will leave this topic of contradiction to the side for now. My existential claim is not unlike saying that I live in a way that is mindful of acting with love. It's all about the experience. It's not about what one reports at the end; it's not what a person has to show when they die.

As I advocate for looking at life as sets of experiences and laughing at each one, I think it's pretty reasonable to think of meaning in the sense of what's relevant to every experience. You could, in the end, bring all your experiences together as a project. But you don't really have to. I decided to live to laugh. With this simple decision, I hope to move on living my life as unencumbered as possible. With this decision, I am also ready to think about how to laugh. I didn't learn that in school, or if they taught the subject, I wasn't paying attention. I have already listed a few things that distracted me during my school years.

What is laughter?

Now that I've established that I'll live to laugh, I want to know what I'm talking about. What is it that I will do? I want to set myself up to laugh in a genuine way. I will distinguish laughter from other nonlaughing activities and from laughing in a way that I don't want to participate in.

SMILING. Laughing is not the same as smiling. Smiling is moving the facial muscles, and it can convey what's in the soul. It communicates peace; it also shares internal joy with others. It can convey safety and trust when the eyes participate. But laughter is a level of joy that is expressed more freely and boisterously; it communicates an elated sense of well-being and excitement. Smiling is a reserved way of expressing the joyful.

The difference is not only of degree but also of kind. With laughter, you let yourself out. You make a noise and externalize yourself, moving air. By smiling, you allow others to see what you're feeling, but you don't go beyond that. A typology of some sort comes to mind. There is the person who doesn't smile at all. They either keep their joy inward or don't even experience it. If you don't share your happiness, others may consider you unhappy. You may choose not to share your sadness either, and if you maintain a deadpan expression, you are just keeping it all in. There is also the person who smiles but doesn't laugh. In doing this, they are communicating a few things. They are sharing that they're not sad at that moment. They are allowing others to see some of their feelings, but they're not communicating strongly or deeply. They display their feelings to the eyes but not the ears. Conversely, the person who laughs creates sound waves that reach far beyond their immediate area. Laughter has a physical impact. You literally change the world around you when you laugh.

I am fascinated by people who laugh out loud. There are also people whose whole body shakes when they laugh. These are my favorite people. However, I am operating within an American/Euro/Arabic culture. It would be interesting to look at laughter in divergent cultures. There is no one correct way to laugh. Can I say that it's universally good to laugh? I am sure that research demonstrates that laughter is good for everyone, but that's irrelevant here. I don't really care. For now, I want to laugh and do so out loud whenever I can.

TRYING TO BE FUNNY. Living to laugh also doesn't mean trying to be funny all the time. I won't even try. Besides, laughing isn't about the joke itself, it's about an attitude and a choice of expression. On the other hand, being funny depends a lot on other people's perceptions. Don't get me wrong, having a sense of humor that's appreciated by others is good and makes laughing easier. But you can laugh without ever telling or hearing a joke. In contrast, you could say the funniest thing (from a particular perspective), but someone else won't get it. You could also say nothing, and another person could die laughing.

Of course, like most people, I enjoy good humor. If I want to laugh, I may try to find humor in a certain situation. My decision to laugh involves looking to find the humor. But I won't wait to laugh until then. I will laugh now.

Also, I don't want to try to be funny when I might worry about failing. I don't want to be jealous of those people who are funny without even trying. There are people whose critical voices I hear in my imagination, telling me this is simply not funny. I have developed strategies to manage these voices, which I will share with you later.

Finding humor is a great way to manage your struggles. It's better than gratitude, in my opinion. As I said earlier, there's something inauthentic about too much gratitude. With gratitude, just like with being positive, you're focusing on only some parts of reality and denying or avoiding other parts. You are selective of what soothes your discomfort. But with humor, you're in a position to deal with both sides simultaneously. With humor, you can say that you don't give a fuck without necessarily sacrificing what you care about. Humor brings the contradictions together.

In *A Love Attempt*, I said that only love can help you accept or manage the paradox of life. I didn't know enough about laughter then. True love brings contradictions to be reconciled, but it's not the only way to reconcile opposing sides. Laughing is far more efficient, actually. However, as I will discuss next, if you bring love into your attempts to laugh, you just might spare yourself some torment.

It saddens me that there is not more room for humor in people's lives. Humor is underutilized and inaccessible to some people. However, in its essence, laughter is a choice you make along the way to find humor. Without this essential choice to let yourself laugh, humor would not work.

THE EVIL LAUGH. I want to laugh, but some specifications are important. Not every laugh counts! There are a few types of laughter that I need to be mindful of and avoid. To me, it's evil to laugh when someone laughs alone or with a group of people at the expense of someone else who doesn't fully consent. In essence, there is a hard divide between me and the other person. The other person being laughed at is excluded from the group and doesn't see the laughter as forming a we/us. They're not enjoying or approving of it. A variation of this is when the "I" distinguishes itself from everyone else (not a specific other). Here, I don't recognize anyone else because I'm so focused on my narcissistic obsessions. I'm celebrating a superiority of some sort and looking down on others. I'm laughing because my achievements give me reasons to believe in my worth after I've had plenty of doubts. That is a kind of laughter I never want to have.

A third kind of evil laugh is when someone enjoys other people's suffering. This person forms relationships with others that lack empathy. Worse, they find a source of amusement in others' misery. Some could say that the person who laughs in these circumstances feels empty inside. One way to feel less miserable and experience a sense of joy is to witness others' misfortune. Since the person feels that everyone is miserable in the same way, they feel less alone in their miserable pit. I'd hate to be in that place of torment and envy.

There is also the case of a potentially more evil source of laughter, and this has an element of each of the types I have just mentioned. This is laughter at the loss of meaning in life. The person laughing in this way comes from a place of extreme anguish. They give up trying to connect to anything they have wanted and perceived as desirable or beautiful, and resort instead to calling what or who they wanted so badly ugly or other bad names. They cloak their reactions with reason. They convince themselves and try to convince others that it's all a delusion; it's just a joke! They might also have done something terrible that is weighing heavily on their conscience, and to relieve the burden, they normalize what they did by claiming that we've all done such terrible things. They celebrate humanity's hypocrisy and find amusement in calling out others' 'delusions.' When naming other people's hypocrisies, they laugh because they find confirmation in their belief that all humans are evil like them. They laugh when they call out a delusion because they feel themselves as the enlightened ones who knew it all along.

This last type of laughter is a mixture of all the previous ones. The person feels superior for having known something earlier or at least does not feel inferior like they would if they were the only hypocrite. They find joy in calling out others and causing hurt or destroying a person's peace. They laugh alone and are miserable.

Punch down. I would never want to be like the person who lumps groups of people together and endlessly rehashes with themselves and their friends with a similar mindset what makes the other group distinct from them. They repeat "jokes" to laugh at and decrease their anxiety about the difference that's no difference. They want to assure themselves that they're not like the other group but superior to them. This pattern of laughter is horribly prevalent, and it's easy to spot. If you're a White, straight, rich male bastard who went to Yale and works on Wall Street, you'd do better to just shut up and never laugh at any joke that involves groups other than yours. Just feel guilty until you wither away and none of you exist. Sorry to break the news to you, but the world would be a better place without you and your kind.

To me, racial slurs, misogynistic and xenophobic references, and laughter at gay people are not okay. Remember that even if you're not that straight, rich Yale guy, you're likely to have privileges related to a few domains of your identity. You could be straight instead of gay. You could be rich as opposed to poor. You could be male or female at birth as opposed to a transgender person. You could have been educated in an elite school as opposed to being publicly educated or getting little to no education at all. You could be American born as opposed to an immigrant from a "third-world" country. You could be White instead of a person of color.

So when an Arab man who can pass as White makes jokes about people with darker skin than him or about countries poorer than his, he is as off-putting in the same way as the White male from Yale. Yes, I'm an immigrant from Syria and have dark skin and speak with an accent. But I'm also a doctor and university professor at a top public university, with a high-earning job. I'm a straight male who passes for White, even though I identify as a person of color. I speak excellent English, and I have other talents. The only identified group I can punch on consists of the bastards I've already mentioned. I could never make fun of a gay person, immigrant, person of color, or poor person. That would just be disgusting. But I also couldn't make fun of a poor, white working-class male with little education and a below-minimum-wage job. Now, can I poke fun at an upper-middle-class woman with a good education and comparable income? That's a tough call. It depends. I could answer "yes" when the Karen's victim is a Black man or a person of color like myself. However, it's questionable when it's about the consequences of the person's life choices; I may not be in a position to poke fun at that. I definitely don't find joking about White women hustling to receive equal pay compared with White men to be appropriate. But I think it is funny and weird as hell that some White women compete for diversity and inclusion positions at educational institutions, elbowing away Black men and women. These White women are only going after a bigger piece of the pie, and once they wrench that away that from the White male, they're keeping it for themselves. Many of them are just as prejudiced as their male counterparts.

LAUGHTER THAT IS A BORDERLINE CAUSE FOR CONCERN.

There is some borderline laughter that I'm okay with using at times but have to be careful not to overdo. It's not evil, but it's also not unproblematic. The first of this type involves compensating for what's lacking in one's life while taking the lived situation as unchangeable. Here, laughter decreases one's level of discomfort, even if the cause of the suffering is untouched. Let's say I have chosen to laugh because my lived experience is terrible. I am okay with that, and it will help me along the way as I manage my situation and turn my life into something more tolerable. In changeable conditions, I'd want to ensure that I'm not stuck in the laughter without doing anything about the circumstances.

I would use this laughter, but I'd pay attention to what I am doing. I'd call it out. I'd have to think about what I am laughing at and whether I could expend some energy trying to turn the situation around.

Laughing about encountered violence is another example of this type of borderline humor. People who are the victim of any form of violence can sometimes tell jokes about their experiences. They are attempting to make peace with what happened to them. I did this when I was beaten up by a teacher, a story I mentioned in my memoir *Being Authentic*. When I recounted the story, I had to bring in some humor to lighten its impact on my soul. It was a traumatic experience, and telling the story is retraumatizing. When I laugh about it, its grip on me loosens and I can move on. But I don't want to focus my humor on the violence I've encountered in my life. I want to laugh by myself and with people about more enjoyable topics. Still, when the memories come, I allow myself to experience whatever remains of the pain and manage it with a bit of laughter without fixating on the situation.

Then, there is laughing to entertain others. Professional comedians are essential, and I am grateful for many of them. For me, some first-class comedians have a status that is close to that of poets, prophets, and philosophers. These four groups employ notions available to everyone around them in a developed way to reconstruct meaning. Prophets are too greedy, and seek to answer the huge questions of life by hijacking what's beyond death. They lure their followers into obsessing with the unknown and play on people's unconscious fears and desires to construct a moral system that, in reality, is flawed, fragile, and unjust. Philosophers are less inclined to try to answer all the questions at once. Still, they provide answers in systems they've developed in their own unique ways. Poets work within systems of meaning to refine language and enhance its sensibility to our experiences. They capture the essence of what's lived and then let it loose in the words and images they use.

Comedians operate at a very concrete level and use language that captures the contradictions and ironies in life. They take us into areas of discomfort through laughter. Of these four groups, my least favorite are the prophets, and the ones I most enjoy are the comedians. In the prophets' attempts to transcend their struggles and break free of the agonies of their generations, they generate closed systems that become the cause of more pain for future generations. Comedians are typically forgotten by the next generation, so they cause less harm.

I haven't trained to be a comedian, and my lived experiences haven't provided the natural conditions for my talent to grow in that arena. I don't aspire to entertain others. I want to be mindful of thinking about laughter in the sense of trying to make others laugh. Yes, I do want to laugh with others, and I want them to experience joy. If possible, I aim to help someone laugh. But what I am presenting here is a system of ideas that I hope will encourage anyone to laugh on their own. I'm not going to be here forever. Making you laugh isn't my job. But laughter is good for you, nonetheless. If we were to establish a religion today, the commandment "Thou shalt laugh" should be included somewhere. But everyone needs to be careful not to become obsessed with making others laugh. Often, what one person finds funny, another does not. The first person should be free to laugh at it. And if the second person doesn't want to laugh, that's their prerogative. Sometimes, one person laughs while someone else doesn't have the bandwidth to do so. I've been in spaces where I was stressed out and couldn't make room for another person's humor or teasing. In those situations, it's nice that you try to make me laugh, but if you don't succeed, please don't take it personally. And please keep laughing without me!

SELF-DEPRECATION. Self-deprecation is about expressing one's own insecurities, for example exaggerating the experience of self-doubt or failure, and exposing it for others to laugh at. This is a powerful way to heal and reconcile. If someone confidently laughs at their struggles and failures, they might be healed by self-deprecation. Sometimes, though, self-deprecation can be problematic. When someone receives approval and laughter from others as a reward for self-deprecation, they might continue their self-deprecation to obtain more approval. But to continue generating material to get the approval they crave, they need to maintain their insecurities and low self-esteem. Otherwise, they would be inauthentic.

True, self-deprecation can invite others into a space of authenticity and vulnerability. It says, "I have done a terrible thing, and I'm laughing at it. I know we all have done that, so let's laugh at it, heal, and move on." But there's also self-depreciation in the awkward sense of digging deep into your own struggle in an experience that's not shared by others or, worse, in an experience of suffering to which the others have contributed. This type of self-depreciation is like making yourself bleed for someone else's amusement. Some may laugh at or with you in such a situation, but empathetic people likely would not laugh at this kind of double suffering; they would only feel awkward.

I do not really enjoy self-deprecating jokes. I just feel that the joke does not apply to me. If I am self-deprecating and become aware of it, I worry others will not relate to my experience. Also, as I said before, I am not a puppet or someone's joker, even though I respect those people who take the role of puppet or joker. I have too much pride to make fun of myself to amuse other people. I don't think I'm better than anyone else, but I'm also not less than anyone either, so I see no reason to make myself vulnerable for other people's amusement.

How to laugh

I have developed one exercise to try to understand how I laugh by making myself laugh and thinking of what happens in the process. First, I start laughing. Then, I close my eyes and take a deep breath. The air comes out of my wind pipes in big bursts at first and then gets smaller and smaller. My stomach goes up and down as I continue to laugh. I take another breath. The next one is a big sigh. I'm preparing for a longer laugh, and I need to fill these spaces that were forced empty with air. I laughed, and it was lovely. It's fun, silly, and nonthreatening. No one is watching me, so I don't need to worry about anything. I'm just here, laughing while I think about laughing.

This is my formula: You decide to laugh, then you laugh, and then you search for the reason why you did so. How many times have you laughed at a joke before hearing it? How many times have you met someone and laughed before even saying a word? Search for a reason to laugh. Pay more attention to any possible humor you can find. To maintain the laughter, push the joy up a notch, and share it with others. Silence your inner critic by calling it out.

I may feel self-conscious doing this exercise. But I tell myself to forget about trying to be funny. Instead, I say to myself, "Be you. And laugh." Laughter is a decision. I allow myself to simply do it. I laugh and then find a reason. Well, I'm drafting a book about laughing, and that's silly as hell. I'm in the fifth round of revisions but still unsure about what I'm doing. I'm nervous about it—that's a good reason to laugh! It's so much fun to just be my silly self for a second. I can only imagine some of my tight-lipped colleagues or family members reading this piece. Gosh, what would they say? "What are you doing, you poor lost soul?" I laugh as I think about it. I silence the critic as I decide to laugh more. I let the laughter take me wherever it goes.

When laughing in this exercise, I became aware of my here and now, and my light heart embraced my insecurity. The anxiety that arises from insecurity is eased by laughter. I then thought about the people who annoy me. I felt the aggravation rise up, but visualizing them in a cartoonish way released the tension. So I laughed more. In my strategies, I set the stage with my laughter to feel safe and secure. Then, I built my tension by feeling insecure, anxious, and annoyed. I then released those tensions by recognizing the silliness of my insecurity, prompting more laughter, and minimizing the annoying impact of others. Throughout this exercise, I continued to feel safe.

Through my sense of humor, I bring myself (and others) close to the edge of a cliff, but I try not to jump or throw them off. I see my insecurity in my annoyance, but I don't dwell on the subject. I do not fall apart. What helps me stay composed is that I am laughing. When I laugh, I am not held hostage by feelings I don't want to control me. If I feel I have pushed myself too far, I regulate my emotions with deep breathing, which is my backup plan for maintaining a sense of calm and safety. But often, laughter alone can help ease the tension. Laughter helps me see something funny in that tension, and that makes me laugh even more.

I want to do something offbeat by bringing in the awareness of my experience and seeing if I can modify one or more elements to make me laugh. I developed a sophisticated framework in the first chapter to deal with experiences. Now is the time to put it to use.

I observe myself writing this book. I am sitting here in the darkness of the room, quiet and barely moving. My butt is glued to the chair, and because I sit sideways, it's mostly my left butt cheek that's squeezed down with the pressure of my weight. My back is forced against the back of the chair. My eyes are focused on the letters on the screen and the cursor as it pulsates. The cursor appears and disappears as if waiting for me to say more. It pleads, "Come on!" It's not a fast-paced flashing, maybe one beat per second or so, just like my heart rate. I wonder if I would think and type faster if the cursor flashed quicker. I hear the noise my fingers make on the keyboard, and in my mind, an image of the critics I've just let go of comes back. It's like they are screaming while the whirlwinds of my thoughts swallow them into the dark matter of my unconscious mind. Enjoy the ride, and take your annoying voices with you!

These are the elements of my writing experience. Can something be made funny here? Let's try! Although I am laughing, I am thinking of an element that I can adjust to make me laugh more. Something that comes to mind is that I am writing this reflection in the second round of revisions, yet I am in the exact same position I was in the first round. I did not change my physical environment. My poor left butt cheek is still glued to the same spot in the chair. I give myself a little pat on the back for perseverance, or what other people might call wasting my time. Now I call my imagination into play. Instead of the letters coming to mind one at a time, why don't whole sentences just emerge on the screen with less effort? I remember a friend who read a piece I wrote and said it was really great. He asked, "Did you hire a ghostwriter?" I wondered if that would make my life easier. It's true that I don't really care much about having my name on books; rather, I'm focused on getting the job done. So why not just go to sleep and let someone else do this work? Laughing is fun. But guess what's more enjoyable? Sleeping. I laugh and decide to go to sleep. I do not hire a ghostwriter; I just get some needed rest.

Let's pause and think about what I did in this last exercise.

As usual, I laughed at the beginning. When I laughed, my mind searched for funny things in my writing about laughing. I found these elements in the irony, tension, and struggle of sitting on my butt for days doing the same task. Part of me wanted to congratulate myself. But as a humble person, I was uncomfortable with the idea of self-congratulation, so I brought myself down a notch by turning my attention to my sore ass! I am a human with a pain in my rear; some may say I am the pain in my own rear, but that's another story! I took the butt image further to include a butt with two cheeks. I wanted to experience talking about my left butt cheek in my book, which created a sense of vulnerability. I felt the release of tension. First, the tension around my self-congratulatory feeling faded after being humbled and laughing about it. Then, the stress of feeling vulnerable was eased by laughing more and moving on.

I attempted next to use my imagination to alter the elements of the experience. In my mind, I imagined words and sentences appearing magically on their own. I quickly thought of another option: hire someone to do my writing. But hiring a ghostwriter who might do an extreme reconstruction of my piece would take the soul out of my work. That's why celebrities' autobiographies read and sound the same to me. I think that hiring a ghostwriter may be unethical too! I bust my ass putting my ideas on paper before editing and revising them. Some rich bastards hire poor kids to write them a piece, and some busy celebrities with little talent or even an interesting story hire someone to do their work, and then they stick their photos on a highly crafted and refined piece of shit that becomes the next best-seller. That's just not fair! Yet, it was funny when that guy asked me whether I used a ghostwriter.

We had just met, and his question made me mad.

I wasn't sure of his intentions. Was he insinuating that I somehow wasn't qualified to write that article, or is he someone who does not choose his best words at times? I laugh as I remember the incident and the ambiguity I felt; it was like sitting on the edge of the cliff. In thinking about it now, I can unpack the whole experience and make sense of it. Or I can simply laugh at it as an experience that I will not burden myself with by exploring any further. It was just odd, to say the least. Now, I laugh even more. My last laugh came as I reflected that I had grown to appreciate this guy who became a friend. He has good taste in clothes and presents himself well professionally. Often, he stops and chats when we run into each other. I know he sees me, and I see him as well, even though he brought me closer to the edge.

It is worth exploring this last realization. As I reflected on this friendship and put into words my and my friend's actions, including his comment that I view now as a tease, I felt my heart warm. Laughter had allowed me first to not be so uptight about the meaning of his comment. Instead, I took it lightheartedly. Then, sitting with the experience and exploring some of its elements allowed me to feel simple human connectedness. That's what I mean when I say we genuinely connect with others when we laugh. We also laugh because we love. Had I chosen to be bitter and harbor mistrust, I would not have been in a position to interpret his comment as his teasing me. Instead, I would have taken it as an attack. Because I laugh, I can appreciate being appreciated.

When it comes to appreciation, the first person we need to appreciate so that we can laugh is ourself. Laughing and enjoying your own sense of humor are authentic expressions. You cannot copy someone else. If you try to, you will only be as funny as the other person, or you will only be funny as long as you are copying them well. In that case, your talent is not being funny; it's being able to imitate others. You need to come up with your own style, something people will recognize as your signature, which is uniquely funny. Value yourself and your style. Sometimes, you can just say your signature phrases and people will laugh. They may roll their eyes too, and that's okay. That's why if I'm really going to teach myself about humor and how to be funny, the first thing to know is how to be funny in my own eyes. Humor is about self-love. It's not necessarily an eccentric task, but you focus on it for your own amusement, which is a way of loving yourself.

Of course, if someone else is involved, humor is also about the other person, and it only works if you care about and love the other person. With humor, you prioritize the other person. Let's go back to the example of the comedians. When comedians say to their fans, "I love you all," the implication is that they prioritize their fans' satisfaction. They work to amuse them and keep them happy. Artists work with love on the thing they are creating, and in doing this, they're authentic. It's important, however, that they learn how to give themselves space and not be so attached to how their audience is receiving them. Everyone yearns for the feeling of being wanted and desired, but not constantly. This is valid in love and everywhere else. Sometimes, I just want the other person to leave me the fuck alone. I want to laugh with them; that's why I maintain my distance from them and between them and my ideas.

Laughing anytime at anything

As I explore what I can laugh about or because of, I start thinking more about what's funny to me. I ask myself the question, "What do I find funny?" I enjoy some jokes that have a structure. They begin with an intro to set the stage. Then they build the tension until finally it gets released with a punch line, and we all laugh. I could also make a funny comment in response to a situation or as a reaction to another comment. The comment would summarize the situation, revealing sides that are unseen and bringing out what is unsaid.

There is also fun banter, in which the back and forth can be funny. Banter may not involve more than one back and forth. However, it often continues and may disrupt an established pattern of conversation between two or more people. I think about the responses in bantering, cranking it up a notch or two higher than normal. This also happens with an answer that obliquely responds to an offer in a conversation but can potentially go to another nonparallel level. Then the punch line can be funny in itself, within a particular context, or completely out of context.

Besides funny jokes and banter, as I encounter what makes me laugh, I can see many things that fall into some broader patterns. For example, inconsistency can be funny. The odd and eccentric are also amusing at times. Moreover, the unexpected can stimulate laughter. What is out of context can be funny, that is, what brings together unrelated elements and reveals hidden or subtle similarities. Anything that threatens to violate norms but still keeps us safe can also be funny. It's important to note that in these instances, there is an implicit assumed *intentionality* about humor or making someone laugh.

Similarly, the accidental nature of certain occurrences can be funny. I keep in mind that an experience has numerous elements, and what's funny about it can be about one or more of those elements. Take, for example, an image. The image can be misshapen, unbalanced, or lacking symmetry, or it may have a component that simply doesn't fit. A shape that has some irregularity or that presents odd relationships can also look funny. So, if I am living an experience and looking at its elements while trying to modify something in order to infuse humor, I could incorporate an element that's odd looking. For example, I could use my imagination and infuse my coffee drinking experience with the silliness of my coffee cup stating, "I love Habermas!" Actually, I have a cup like that. It's a gift from one of my dear friends. Whenever I use it, I laugh. It reminds me how much I have used quotes from Habermas in my conversations with this friend. It's as if he was saying, "you seem like you love Habermas a little too much; I got you a cup to save you breath!"

When I interact with someone, for humor to be created, I hope that they do something unexpected and unusual, challenge my norms, or intentionally violate an expectation. That would make my heart drop for a second and might trouble my mind until I realize, hopefully, that they're just being silly. They could also tell a story with odd elements. It would be so much fun if they came up with the story on the spot or modified some elements to make it more interesting. Sometimes, people complain about falsified elements of a story and beg for honesty. I would say that perhaps humans are generally too honest and literal when they tell stories. By injecting some humor, you can add and remove irrelevant details. Hopefully, the audience will get the hint that it's a joke and not be expecting a news report. They will know that the person is not blatantly lying. There is humor in stretching the elements of the lived experience a little.

Remember, it's all about the experience, and within that experience, always get in touch with what's going on with you. It's not about describing what's happening around you, and it's not only about the incident. What matters is how the experience involves people. You encounter a world of experience with your senses—through hearing, seeing, smelling, tasting, and touching. You also meet experience in how you let yourself respond to it emotionally. You may feel sad, annoyed, angry, or happy about it. You also engage with experience in how you think about it and what you remember about it. You can even go further to speak about those elements that trigger the mental aspects of your worldview, culture, opinions, and numerous other aspects. Don't limit yourself! All these elements are modifiable and can be altered to create humor in the story you tell, even if only in your own head.

But what are the limits? This is the hardest question to answer. If you're sharing what makes you laugh with others, be mindful of the impacts of your words. Everyone operates within social contexts that have their own norms. There are some rigid expectations of performance in specific spaces. Let's say you're in a relationship and your partner dislikes certain kinds of jokes or comments that other friends of yours don't mind. You will have to make a choice. Maybe you can get an allowance from your lover, say, two bad jokes a week. But it gets harder when there are rigid expectations or consequences. Let's say that your profession isn't amenable to certain types of funny remarks. For example, I find humor that blurs the boundaries between doctors and patients as wildly inappropriate, and I feel uncomfortable when I'm invited or pushed to participate in such humor.

Causing discomfort can be an indicator of trespassing boundaries. The tricky part about humor, though, is that it quickly disarms you. Someone can laugh out loud while saying evil things, but what if their intention is supposedly to be humorous? You will have to promptly make a decision. Do you just not participate and maintain a stern face? Or do you take it up a notch by saying, "That's not funny!" You could even push back more by stating, "That's not acceptable!" Or even more forcefully saying, "Stop!" or "You owe me an apology!" All these options are available. We can cause damage with our jokes, and we're responsible for the humor we use.

We need to be mindful of how people can exploit humor to get their own way. They may laugh and try to get you to laugh when they ask a question with a wink, as if implying you are hypocritical or hiding something. As I develop the capacity to laugh, I must also build my capacity to stop laughing. When I maintain a stern face, I can choose from a few actions. I don't have to participate in the plot the other person has "strategically" laid out. At the same time, I could monitor my feelings and regulate the flow of my thoughts before I participate in laughing, if I don't want to, by conjuring up a dark image—maybe a kitten being tortured by an evil human. Then I can say it explicitly, "stop, you're torturing the cat!"

Laughing with style

I always remind myself that when I laugh, I am being me. The problem with writing about laughter, however, is that people may expect me to be laughing all the time. If that is the case, there will be pressure, just like with any performance, and I could risk losing myself along the way. But do I really need to feel this pressure? The fact that people expect something from you doesn't have to affect you unless you allow it to. The essential inner work here involves worrying less about what people expect of you or want from you. It's about giving up the desire to please people when their expectations are grounded in their own wishes and desires. Sometimes, what people want from you is to be consistent with what they think is you! They want you to fit into their mental framework. It seems that it's painful for people to perceive and accept an outside reality that is not in line with their framework. Guess what? The world isn't going to be exactly the way you want it to be, or imagined it would be, so you would be better off giving up the desire to control it to be the way you want.

Because there is the risk of pressure and worry about not being myself through my writing about laughter, I need to develop mechanisms to deal with the risk. I need to be able to neutralize others' expectations. They're not authorized to control me or anyone else, for that matter. I don't need to make anyone happy; happiness is each person's own responsibility. I don't need anything from anyone as a gift or an act of grace. I am independent, a free soul, and I am not compelled to do anything I don't want to do. I am in control and the one who decides what or what not to do. But I am not a control freak when it comes to people's perceptions of me. Those other people were just there and said a few words, but those words don't need to bother me. People can say whatever they want; it's just words. I am here doing what I want. I will laugh at the whole situation after naming it. And I will breathe deeply to keep my emotions in balance. Then I will move on.

Also, because when we laugh we externalize ourselves, there is a level of awkwardness in putting ourselves out there. In any act of expression, whether it's dancing, singing, talking, or even showing up for others, the awkwardness comes from self-doubt and questioning whether our efforts are good enough. Laughing is not unlike entering any space of discomfort. I was at a lounge, and a beautiful lady invited me to dance with her. I was reluctant at first, but then I decided to dance with her even though I was terribly self-conscious. I had to develop a system by which I recognized that the burden of not putting myself out there was much greater than the ordeal of being out on the floor dancing. I have developed my personality to be able to take such risks. I have a strong normative position that I think I inherited from my mom: "You should go out there and dance," she would have said. Still, I struggle with the sense of discomfort that arises when I engage in this activity. It's a feeling of being in an empty space where all eyes are glaring at me. I laugh at this intensity and carry on dancing.

Frameworks such as "I don't care because I am better than anyone else" don't work very well as neutralizers. They are childish and dumb. No one is better than anyone else. You have to come up with something better. Other frameworks include: "I am the king of my own world." "I am good enough at this." "I am getting better." "I am learning to do this." Anyone can make the same mistakes in the same situation; it's okay. Most people probably don't really care. The only ones who do care are those controlled by envy, and they are to be pitied. Most people won't even see or remember this, after all. If they remember, they might tease me some, but I can laugh and handle it. On the other hand, some people genuinely care about, love, and support me. What I do is just for fun. It's an attempt, and the next time will be more developed. If they poke fun in a mean way, I can set my boundaries with those bullies. All of the framework phrases mentioned above are appropriate, and I will use them.

You can memorize all the frameworks and shift from one to another. Some will be more effective than others in different situations. Some will give you the boost of confidence you need at a particular point in time. I will use them when I decide to make a funny remark but worry how others will receive it. I hope I won't need to do that very often, however. Laughter is about safety. I want to make the spaces around me safe and find the safe spaces to inhabit where I can be authentically me.

Another expectation I need to manage concerns the frequency of laughing. Living to laugh has to be done with style. One aspect of this is the idea that laughter has to be meted out at the right moment. I go back and forth between thinking, "You can't just laugh the entire time" and "You should laugh as much as you want and can!" In resolving this issue, my therapist came to mind. It felt like anytime we peeled back a layer of discomfort, she would find something else to poke at. I think my answer to the question of frequency is that I will choose to laugh whenever and as often as I want. There is no right moment for laughter; it can be in every moment. As long as I am living, struggling, and loving, I have material to laugh about!

But I have my own style of laughing. I first take myself and consenting others into a space of discomfort. Then, I bring them back to the space of laughter. This is the basic idea. Laughter is letting loose the tension of being stressed and uptight. It's like music that holds the tension until being released at the end with joy. So, when I say I want to be laughing the whole time, I do not mean I expect to be happy or joyful the entire time. I need to encounter all my true feelings, including sadness and anger, and I need to be in spaces of discomfort in order to laugh. So technically, I cannot be bursting out in laughter in every moment. I will have to stop sometimes to get the fuel for my laughter from my pain. But I also don't have to live a bipolar experience. The rhythm of my laughter can be naturally interrupted and changed. There are no rules that don't need to be broken at times, including the one that states, "All rules must be broken at times!"

How will I ensure that I'm not self-critical when I read what I have written here? How do I know that when I edit this again, I'll find it humorous? Well, it's not going to be funny the whole time. It has to be funny from some perspectives, and it is important to develop some criteria for what's funny. It also has to be authentically me and to come with love. You might sometimes say something you think is funny, and then you come back and judge it as terrible. Your mood has shifted, and that's okay. But how will you know if the second judgment is valid but the first one isn't? Maybe you could learn to take different positions around it. For example, "If I were excited and feeling joy, how would I judge this subject?" and then, "If I were feeling the blues, how would I judge this subject?" When I am excited and filled with joy, I tend to be exuberant and expressive and to find harmony and acceptance. I have more space to tolerate others. But when I am down, I tend to judge things more negatively and say no more often. I need to become conscious of these variations in my perceptions and learn to be kinder to myself. And so do you.

Learning is always possible. The question will arise often of how you can ensure that what you say is funny. You can't. You do what you think is funny in the moment and then let go. You simply move on; you don't ponder what you've done or allow the awkwardness of the moment to affect your subsequent actions. Most often, people don't even notice your awkwardness. Know your boundaries, and know the conditions in which you may be at risk of crossing your boundaries. Stay within your lane, but don't overthink it.

What stops me from laughing?

Sometimes, I may hold off letting myself laugh. Sometimes, laughing can mean a person is not dealing with other serious emotions. Someone who chooses to laugh might find joy in the experience of laughing in order to avoid more difficult feelings. These feelings become suppressed into transient whims the person learns to quickly process. This is dangerous. However, I think this worry can be addressed if the person allows the time and space to check on their feelings. Also, suppose one is using humor to deal with difficult emotions. In that case, there must be time to deal with these emotions and the experiences provoking them, even if gradually and slowly. The person needs to allow the space to feel anxiety and fear. There's no need to be controlled by sadness, but when it comes, it should be welcomed just like any graceful visitor.

Laughter and moving on versus lingering with a subject and unpacking it can be compared to making a quick pass versus taking time to think something through. I am choosing to default to a fast way to judge the situation and to use humor to do this. This does not mean I give up developing the capacity to be thoughtful. Actually, I've already developed this capacity—I have done plenty of that already. I exercised it in writing this book and my three previous ones. I would say that developing the ability to deal with complexity may be necessary for someone to be able to laugh and not cause too much damage.

Then, there is the fear of not being thought of as a serious person because of one's choosing to laugh. So far in my life, I have occupied positions in society that require a particular way of presenting myself to people. If I change the way I show up, others may worry about my capacity to perform my tasks. They may even begin to worry about my well-being. I worry about becoming insane and losing it entirely. Losing it can mean simply not having the ability to present myself in my usual way. It can also mean not having the emotional presence to appear with a composed demeanor. The consequences, however, are losing the trust and confidence of others. That's why I called it earlier "laughing with style." I can be reasonable with my actions based on the situation and context. At the same time, some of my serious contexts may benefit from laughter too. I can afford to take some risks.

I need to reframe the subject so that I can start laughing more. It's blatantly wrong to tell someone, "laugh less!" or "you should not laugh!" It's quite concerning to hear, "I actually don't like laughing!" or "I cannot laugh!" When I look around at people who don't laugh, I can identify a few categories. One of these is the miserable person. Life has been very bad for them, and they can't think of a way out. They are the ones who deal with guilt from harming others. They are also the victims who are stuck in victimhood; they simply do not feel anything else but their pain. These people are stuck between victim and perpetrator; failing to heal this dichotomy is what makes it harder for them to laugh.

I know that I am responsible for my actions, and if I caused harm to others, I'd stop, recognize my mistake, and apologize. I refuse to be a victim. Because I am recovering, I will laugh. I laugh to heal. I also have to watch out for those situations when I'm burdened by too much and then prompt myself to laugh. The requirement to laugh can cause extra pressure. Yet, even in these situations, I can still laugh. I start with the mechanical action of moving my facial muscles and pushing the air out of my lungs. Practice this. Then, I move on to laughter and restoring some ease to the situation. I will not take myself too seriously. I will also surround myself with lighthearted people with whom I can share laughter.

Letting go is liberation

my lived experiences are shaped by given elements in the world that I can often change and by positions I take that I can stop adhering to. I could simply remove some of these elements or remove myself from them. I have the means to modify big chunks of the claims I make about my worlds. I obviously have privileges, including holding this same belief about my ability to change. Others who hold opposing positions might have encountered the outside world in different ways. Still, unless you're in a windowless prison, the rising sun can be part of your life if you choose to get up early. Sitting with the discomfort you feel as you hear other's perspectives is a choice.

Letting go is also a choice.

I have long wanted to think of myself as a rational being. Thus, I needed a good reason to alter the elements of my experience. I tried to maintain flexibility. I would name my position and then explore my reasons for taking that stance. I would develop a counterargument and then synthesize a more elaborate position to create something I saw as more valid. But at times, I had to reshape the experience with what felt like a leap of faith. Many people who leave their countries to immigrate and integrate into new societies do just that. When I decided to move to the United States, I didn't have enough information, nor did I have the capacity to comprehend what was facing me. This leap of faith is essential to move forward and move on.

Although they might appear absurd from certain perspectives, many actions based on leaps of faith are not magical. They can be explained with good reasoning. There is an extensive reservoir in our shared culture of meanings we lean on without being aware of them when moving from one position to another.

Quite often, we change our positions, and only then do we come up with the views to support our decisions. In a sense, our mind has done the work before our awareness allowed for sets of arguments to make a case for the change. We shift our positions, which means we let go of our old ones. We take new positions, or at times, we take a break from making new ones. What matters most for me is the act of letting go of a position. That's what I want to master. Today, I want my position to be that "I love to laugh; thus, I will let go!"

The experience of letting go is not new to any of us. We do it all the time.

WE LET GO OF THINGS. We all have objects we like and value, such as our cars, phones, and computers. We've used and enjoyed them for some time. But there comes a point when we must replace them with other objects. We may need a newer and faster computer to replace the one that has slowed down and crashes a lot. We may choose to operate our devices differently. For example, we might want to develop a healthier pattern of using our smartphone. Hence, we give up some phone use time or stop using a particular app.

WE LET GO OF IDEAS. We adopt frameworks and ideas that answer one or several questions. But over time, we find that we have developed new frameworks. Intentionally or unintentionally, we seek alternative frameworks. Some call it soul searching. Here, the goal is to find systems of ideas that help us live with the fewest contradictions, or to find notions that help us manage our contradictions.

WE LET GO OF FAMILY. Siblings and parents exist in each other's lives until it's time to no longer coexist in the same physical space. People have to make choices about how their lives will proceed, and transitions happen, with or without grace. We let go of patterns of being together. It can be hard at first. But time is the best healer, and we get used to a new way of being without them so closely in our lives.

WE LET GO OF FRIENDS. We create bonds with the people we bring closely into our lives. They become our good friends. Suddenly, we realize that our values and theirs are like night and day. Then we naturally want to move on and find new people with whom to associate. Friendships are secular in the sense that we consciously develop them, and we can end them, too. To lay the foundation for a new relationship, we may have to end other friendships or invest less time in them. When we invest less time, some friendships will begin to fizzle. Although it's rarely intentional, we can observe that, over time, the connection has downgraded from a weekly or bimonthly face-to-face visit to a once-a-year text.

WE LET GO OF LOVE AFFAIRS. We develop attachments to people with whom we feel a special affection. We may love someone deeply and seek to have them intimately in our lives. But maybe they decide to find their happiness with someone else. How long do we put our efforts into trying to win back their love? It is better for us to move on and open our hearts to someone else.

WE LET GO OF ACTIVITIES AND HABITS. We tend to do certain things at particular times, and we like to have a routine. Think of the activities you were doing a few years ago and how you're only doing some of them today. Some people manage to intentionally add exercising to their routine. Some decide to stop drinking alcohol. We constantly shift our activities and behaviors, and we set up a structure around ourselves to maintain our new habits. When we incorporate new habits, we let go of others.

WE ALSO LET GO OF LIFE. We are all going to die. Many people we've known have already died. Some among us are lucky enough to be able to select the time and mode of our death. Here, I mean dying with dignity. Others fight it. People try to reconcile the idea of death. But for most people, this is not an urgent task. You let go of thinking about it. It's not like you get to choose to die or not die. You'll deal with it when it comes. Then, you die, and with that, you let go of living.

As I mention these examples, it all sounds so easy. True, we do it all the time, but it can be extremely difficult. Because it's so hard and because dealing with circumstances that can be better dealt with by letting go brings about a fierce struggle, this space creates fertile ground for laughter! When we struggle, we feel the heaviness of the burden. Laughter lightens the load. We also feel anxious, fearful, and maybe angry. Laughter helps to break us out of those feelings and release the tension.

However, the journey of laughing and letting go is not a walk in the park. What is already hard enough in changing ideas and positions gets much harder when it comes to human relationships and connectedness. Letting go of an attachment we've had for someone we loved and cared for is tough. So is letting go of missing our loved ones who are gone. This difficulty has made many people blame attachments for their suffering, and they subsequently choose to stay aloof and disconnected from the world to protect their hearts. This is valid reasoning. The only way to never encounter heartbreak is to not let yourself love. But when you don't love, you suffer from a peculiar kind of misery—existential loneliness. Feeling alone and living in loneliness can make life not worth living.

I disagree with the idea that the root of suffering is attachment. For me, it is an attachment gone rogue that causes the pain. Misery comes when a person has not mastered the ability to manage attachments.

Having an attachment simply means allowing yourself to feel the pain of enduring life without those beings we are attached to. Attachment manifests in the desire to connect and in suffering/pain when without it. There is joy and pleasure in being close to whom we are attached; there is pain and suffering in being away from this person.

Attachments do not happen just with the people in our families; we are also attached to coworkers, friends, and romantic partners, to name just a few. It's true that in our modern life, we often limit ourselves to smaller circles, such as working with the same people. Some people in their forties still have only their high school friends. There is personal meaning and benefit in developing new attachments.

We always need new connections. We form new associations of all kinds as we move through life; we need the capacity to embrace the new in our lives. And it is important to continually refresh and renew our important attachments. People frequently move from one geographic location to another. Friends move on with their lives, leaving others behind. People we love and value die. We also shift the nature of our connections over time. We inevitably change; some like to think of it as evolving (but it's not always!). We make critical choices at specific points in our lives and move on with these. At times, we view ourselves in a particular light and desire to live in a certain way. However, we cannot do so because what we want is not available or we're stuck with a group of people who view the world differently and pressure us to be someone other than who we want to be. In that case, we may have to move on and change our community. We cannot form new attachments if we are still fully occupied with the old ones.

We have to navigate the finite time we have available to us. There are limited hours in the day. If we want to get to know someone and develop our liking for them and accept what we do not like in them, we have to spend time with them in a variety of settings. Suppose you're occupied with objects or people to the extent that you're not open to developing new attachments. In such a situation, you are stuck in your old web of existing relationships. To allow room for the new to enter your life, you cannot hoard old ties. You have to let go.

Along the path of struggle, when you are dealing with opposing positions or conflicts about the direction you want to move in, not only do you suffer, but you sometimes make others struggle with you. You go back and forth. You sense a betrayal of your old self in relation to others. You feel you're not yourself. You have mixed feelings of sadness and anger. You might get a glimpse of joy only to quickly feel guilty for experiencing it. You're stuck, and you might hurt others in your conflicted transition. That's why I want to let go with grace. I want to look back and recognize what was meaningful and enjoyable about the past. I want to say thank you as I move on. I do not want to harbor guilt or regret.

Letting go also means disengaging. To let go, you need to have the space to process and make sense of things. It's not easy to process and let go without having that space. At times, people might come to you and pressure you to participate. They seem to do this at weird times as well. For instance, imagine it's Friday afternoon and you've just clocked out of work when you receive a text from a coworker about a trivial work matter they feel anxious about. You will need to set your boundaries. Letting go means you set your boundaries and know when to say no. It's easier when you stick to your no and hold to it. Often, this means rigidity, but it also means you're maintaining your internal peace. You're making it easier to manage the situation in question.

You also create parameters for what you can and cannot do. You may ask, "Why is it so hard for me to manage a few things?" Then, you recognize that you are overwhelmed. You've been trying to do an extraordinary number of things, and now you're stressing out. Letting go is a way to manage that stress.

Sometimes, you may find spaces for your amusement or even for celebration as you spin the subject around. You dodged a bullet. Dodging a bullet makes you laugh so hard because you're still alive! It's the celebration of a life that wasn't lost. It's the celebration of time that wasn't wasted and the joy that comes from that. We are relieved of the pressure weighing down on our chests. We feel lighter, and our hearts are filled with pure joy.

Letting go with grace

Not responding to a text in order to sever a connection isn't the only way to let go. Quite often, you'll want to let go while expressing gratitude. I have developed the practical steps to achieve this. When I let go of the person, I think about the start of the experience. I also think about the growth and change in the experience. I then think about the context of its ending, recognizing why it started and what it did for me. I evaluate what was done well and what could have been done differently. I practice gratitude. Then, I let go with grace.

Let me build on the example I shared before about my interaction with my therapist. I spoke about my experience with therapy in the context of laughing in order to resist and heal. However, the story had other aspects that I intentionally omitted. After the incident I mentioned regarding my therapist's remark about violence, I resolved to let go of that relationship with grace. In the end, I realized that the therapist had done her best to be caring and supportive.

I was intentional in the process. First, I thought about the reason I had started therapy. I went ahead with it at a time when I was dealing with various sorts of struggles: interpersonal, health issues, grief, and job difficulties, among others. I had assessed my various needs and reminded myself of what I wanted to achieve. I mostly wanted to work with a woman therapist I could trust because I thought she would reflect a common feminist perspective. I was concerned about maintaining the best relationship possible with my partner, whom I had grown to love, and I needed a sounding board I could trust.

After that, I reflected on what was achieved in the interaction. By that time, we had accomplished a lot. I had come to know myself better. I had worked on the wounds from my childhood and adolescence. I had developed new rules for dealing with people while being respectful and mindful. I also had developed strategies to recognize where my tension lies, verifying that my frame of reference works.

Next, I assessed the failings or limitations of that time with my therapist. It was difficult for me to fully participate because of limited time and space. The mental work was stifling my energy. The therapy also took me to places I didn't need to go. It did not help me in my primary goal of keeping the relationship. True, it was a complex relationship, but the desired outcome was not achieved, and the relationship ended.

After that, I identified the areas where I would need similar support, such as in my career, maintaining my mental health and stability, and inspiring me creatively. I counted my sources of support if I stopped going to therapy. I'd be relying on friends and family. I'd have one or two 30-minute talks with people I trust on different subjects to give me a good foundation of reason. I'd find mentors. I thought to myself, I *must* find mentors who can help me and see me as a person. I needed people who could call me out and challenge me. I also needed friends who could do that.

I also explored how I would maintain my mental health. This would include trying to keep a mellow, balanced mood, not too sad and not too excited. I would maintain my energy levels so as not to become hyper and fatigued. I needed to be able to rest as part of maintaining a healthy lifestyle. I planned to exercise three times a week and eat nutritious meals three times a day. I determined to take walks in nature and engage in outdoor activities. To fulfill my social needs, I would enjoy time with friends and family and connect with my community.

I let go of my therapy.

The therapist was someone who helped me and listened to me. Yes, she was professional and got paid, but she did her job with care. It was a meaningful connection. I grieved some. I was a bit sad, actually, but I let go. And I moved on.

The steps I listed above are an extraction for what I intentionally did. I extracted the steps after the fact, but I have gone through this exercise before, and the next time, I will go through it even more efficiently. Now, I will rethink the subject and see how I could let go of the therapist using humor. Here's the process again: Begin with laughing and deconstruct the experience. Silence the critic. Exaggerate. Point out the tensions, jokes, and irony. Repeat.

At the time, my life was upside down. Someone I loved didn't reciprocate my affection, and my life was burdened with stress. I was full of grief, all kinds of grief. You name it, I had it. I went to a therapist, and she was lovely. I was paying out of pocket, but I didn't mind the money part until I noticed the bill. I was paying almost half my fucking monthly mortgage for someone to talk to me for an hour a week! Because many of my friends were therapists, I decided to pocket the money and live a less crazy life. I guess one incentive to not be mentally ill is the cost it entails getting better! You will pay for it in one way or another. So you better get your life in shape. The turning point, though, was when I received a "philosophical scolding" from my White woman therapist when I expressed my struggle to understand White women's perceptions. I said to myself, "I'm paying $750 a month to hear this?" I was done.

Yet, I went for one more appointment to say thank you, not to show her that I'm a kind person but because that is really me and that's how I want to be. I choose to treat others with grace and want to continue doing so. I am capable of treating others with love when I have the bandwidth. I want to maintain enough bandwidth to treat others with care, so I will find strategies to do that.

How to let go by laughing

By now, I hope you get the core hypothesis of this book. Laughing is intertwined with letting go in an existential sense. We laugh more when we let go because our souls are less burdened. We let go more easily when we laugh because our souls are lighter. With humor, you can potentially hold opposing positions. You can stare down the pain. You can live through the struggle. You can hold what initially seems like contradictory positions, wanting the impossible, being afraid of the imminent, feeling helpless with continued losses, or feeling hurt by caring too much. Laugh at the peak of your sense of conflict. You can then move on to a position you believe is authentic for you. You can let go of whatever you want to.

I laugh, and I take advantage of my humor. Laughter allows me to let go of the pain in my lived experiences. It allows me to be inconsistent and manage my inconsistency with care. Only humor can make sense of the contradictions in my life. I can be this way and the opposite because I am joking—or not. I can escape, making a commitment to a notion because I can laugh and be free to commit or not.

Humor and laughter open the space for the crazy to emerge. Gosh, I so much want to be crazy. I am tired of my sanity. I'm tired of being reasonable. I need to break down. I cannot bear the burden of holding it all together anymore. With humor, I can flirt with madness and with all that I consider unreasonable. I can play with alternatives and laugh about potential losses. I can be me as I let go of what I've held on to so tightly that it has burdened me. I am just a person, and what is happening to me is overwhelming. I want space to laugh and be crazy. That's when I let go methodically, and the following are the steps I take that you can apply to your own lives.

First, state your position; then, declare your counter-position. Laugh and then state the arguments for your position and those for the counter-position. Continue to laugh throughout this process. Remind yourself that other people have the counter-position and also that the right position may not be the same over time. You have given up positions you thought were essential at particular times. Laugh. Think of how your life would be if you let go of the positions you've held onto. What are the other positions you need to adjust? State those as well. Laugh some more. Think of the absurdity of life and how these positions really do not matter at all when death comes. Laugh even more. Imagine the beauty and meaning you will have if you let go of your position. Now laugh louder.

Affirm to yourself that you choose your stance on subjects because you can. Think about the double absurdity of spending your time on this same subject. At the same time, you could be okay with the counter-opinion. Laugh to yourself because you will be okay either way. Let go of the need to change your position. Let go of the question altogether. Come to the subject at another time, remembering what you laughed about. Then let go. Move on, remind yourself that you can go back and laugh whenever the pressure returns. Repeat the exercise if you need to. But most importantly, let go and laugh, over and over!

Remember that this applies to most of your positions that relate to what you want and what you consider good and right. It also applies to those frameworks you put in place to understand your experiences. Furthermore, it applies to everything metaphysical, literally everything. Although it may not immediately apply to ideas about the world around us, such as if the earth is round, questioning that truth is not absurd. You could be a social scientist dealing with the idea metaphorically or you could be someone triggering your imagination while high on a psychedelic. You do not need to let go of the scientific view of the world, but the scope of its application needs to be examined and developed.

Learn to let go of your fixed positions. You will then live more lightly and laugh more.

LETTING GO OF THE PAINFUL. I have applied the notion of letting go to a relationship with a person. Can I also use it with those experiences that haunt me? Here is a real challenge: Can I let go of my wounds? I have visited the subject numerous times, and I go back to it as my safety blanket. Like many people with trauma who define themselves by those past events, I am tempted to say, "Pity me; I'm a poor baby. I was maltreated."

Can I just let go of this story? Can I move on and be done with it? I am bored with these stories. There are, of course, good reasons to move on. Ruminating on these events are really not worth one's time. I keep revisiting my wounds, and whenever someone hints at an experience that is related to my trauma, I am triggered. Because I focus on my wounds so much, I find myself limiting the space in my head for the enjoyable moments I have had in the past. Sometimes, I cannot even access the joyful moments I have experienced because they have become buried in a web of pain and agony. Yes, this and that experience was painful. But am I really in pain now because of *them*? Even then, I was mounting the strength to continue. I cried and was hurt, and I suffered for a while. But do I want my psyche today to be defined by those moments?

These difficult experiences are endless. If I finish unpacking one, the next will emerge. And as I finish unpacking that one, the third will appear. And this will continue relentlessly. If I unpack and entirely forget some of my most painful experiences, what would happen? I probably would look for what I would now consider less painful events and agonize over those. I would search for the pain and latch onto it. This has to stop. I need an efficient way to look at the past, unpack it, laugh at it, and move on. I need to examine other areas of my life that are enjoyable and focus on them.

Part of me wants to linger in the moment and sit with these events. I want to describe the experience, recognize it, and feel it. I want to unpack it, explore it, and understand it. But really? Can I genuinely understand an experience from the past in a meaningful way? I can barely understand something that happened to me last week, let alone something that happened to me 20 years ago. I am trying to reconstruct an experience that's not really relevant today. I let go because this attempt lacks validity.

I move on because there is more to life than dwelling in the past. For example, there is this new book that I'm writing now, and I'm almost done with it. It will take a lot of revisions and rewriting, but I accept that. It will come together eventually. I move on with laughter because I don't want to let difficult experiences beat me down. There are some evil people out there, and yes, I can still try to move on with grace. True, the ones who are not doing their work to protect others from their harm are lazy bastards. Yet, I am going to laugh at them and not let their shit stain me. I want to live life joyfully.

In the previous iteration of this book, I went into the details of what is causing me pain. I named the context. I spent time with the feelings. I went on and on pointing out the inconsistencies. But as I read through it, I decided to take that section out. To make the task easier, I created a file I call "extras."

Deep inside, I know this file will just stay there, and I will never look at it again. But it is easier for me to cut and paste what I do not want into that file as opposed to deleting those items off the bat. I know my editors want me to include stories that the readers can relate to. But fuck the editors and fuck the readers! What you hear is my story, and I am living it as I share it at this exact moment. My story today is what you sense between the lines. I let go of amusing people by digging through the wounds of my past.

Instead of going on and on, I decided to stop. I don't care anymore about stating the problem or describing the incidents. My previous trauma is now trivial to me. When I let go, I'm lighter and not bothered by it. It remains as a trace of a long-ago past. I laugh at it and move on. Yes, I am laughing. I am done!

I spoke of letting go of what gives pain. Of course, feeling joy is not something I want to let go of unless I have to for the sake of someone I love or out of duty. Often, these two reasons give me more joy, so I am not worried. I want to let go of my anger and sadness. I tend to feel anger when norms are violated, and I tend to feel sad when my expectations and hopes are not met. I need a strategy to manage these two feelings. First, laugh! Believe me, it's so good to laugh and be here. So let the air out in bursts from your lips with a smile on your face. Check your eyes to make sure they're smiling, too. You don't want only your lips to smile; that would make you look like an evil soul. Laugh and laugh and laugh. It doesn't have to be loud or hysterical, just enough to hear the sound of your breath and make a dent in the air.

Remember, these feelings of anger and sadness are triggered in specific contexts. Managing the feeling is not isolated from managing the experience that provoked it, even though work needs to be done on resolving the feeling itself. That's why when I feel particularly angry or sad, I try to name what is troubling me. In an abstract sense, I am bothered by people who violate the norms and values expected of us all. I am also saddened by those who fail to live up to my hopes and expectations. For example, I was disappointed by a friend who offered to help but didn't follow up when I accepted the offer.

When I shared my breakup with him, he said to text him if I needed support and that he would hold a space for me. I tried to reach out repeatedly, and there was zero response. I felt sad. Then, I thought about it some more. He paid me lip service, and maybe the empathy he expressed was simply pity. That made me mad. I pushed my feelings to the limit in exaggerated grief and anger. Then, I burst out laughing and decided to let it go.

If what provoked the feeling is part of a pattern, I'd turn my back and move on. I "bracket" the friendship and "shrink" how much space I give the person in my mind. I might even announce the end of the relationship and laugh some more. I would open the space in my soul for something different to enter by seeking new gratification and meaningful new friendships. I would reflect on my feelings and decide if what happened was worthy of my sadness and anger. If it was not, then I would start laughing at my silly self. If it was, I'd say, well, too bad! Then, I would move on.

LETTING GO OF PEOPLE AND DEATH.

Even with the annoying people I'd like to open the door to so I can slam it behind them, I still want to let go with grace. If you feel this tension, there might be someone triggering your discomfort. You could simply choose not to deal with this individual, now or ever. The person may be someone you just met and with whom you haven't even developed an attachment. If you let go of this connection, you free up more space in your life to breathe easy and enjoy living. There also could be the bumpy friendship. If you see that this person is not kind to you or others, it might be to your benefit to just dump them.

Do you really need to protect every relationship? Let them go, and laugh about it. You may worry that if you keep doing that, you will feel the pain of loneliness. But actually, there is clarity in being by yourself. Sit with this loneliness and manage your discomfort. At the end of this exercise, you will have opened up the space in your mind to do other things that are meaningful to you. In my life, I prefer to hold the position that these might be beautiful people, but maybe we just didn't vibe together. I want to be able to say thank you and to wish the person good luck. I may not need to have a breakup conversation in all cases, but I should be prepared with a few kind phrases. I have usually been content to just ghost away or turn a weekly walk into something that happens once every few months.

Although I could walk away from a new relationship, there are people in my life I will never be able to fully walk away from. I was born into a family, and I will die holding a place of care for all of them. However, there are some conversations that every family seems to have, whether about politics, COVID-19, or history, that, frankly, I don't care to hear. I just want to be left alone for the time being to manage my life. I want to let go of the family time that I do not want to participate in. I will just attend what is meaningful to me and share pleasant time with my family. On our weekly Skype family meetings, I will choose to silence the upsetting conversation and turn my video off. I can breathe or listen to music until they talk about something else. Or I might say goodbye and carry on with my day.

There is also the letting go of my recent love affair. For a few months after our breakup, I missed her badly and felt a strong urge to see her. But even as I think of her and how much I miss her, I also remember the futility of trying to mend our relationship. Even in the weeks before our breaking up, I sensed her growing apart from me. She was really never in it, and I had to work very hard to maintain the connection. It was her choice to leave. I want to let go of her in the same graceful way I choose to let go of others in my life.

In letting go of these people, there were moments when I felt despair. I was afraid that if I left this or that connection, I'd be alone and lonely, living a depressing life. When I sat with this fear, I could see how my mind was turning the simple letting go into much more. Instead of letting go of the relationship with my ex, it was pushing me to let go of every relationship. I could have stopped this thinking and called it dysfunctional, but I wanted to see what had triggered me.

What the letting go of these relationships had triggered was really my fear of dying alone. My illness—stage 4 lung cancer—snapped into focus. I've already established that I'm afraid of dying and do not want to die. Dying alone, with no one around, seems like the most terrible form of dying to me. The other fear that was triggered was around dealing with other people's deaths. I have encountered death in my life, and someone leaving my life can feel like that person isn't alive anymore. I've lost my mom and sister, and their deaths were very painful to me.

You might say that I don't need to see someone to know they are alive. After all, we all have people in our lives whom we only see rarely or occasionally. But there is always the notion that those people are only a phone call or plane ticket away. But the person who is here and closed off is not really here—they're dead in my mind.

This exercise helped me recognize that letting go of people in my life is closely related to how I deal with death, so I decided to bring death to the forefront. Although I know fully well that the person I'm letting go of isn't really dead, when I decide to let go completely, it means that I may never see that person again until they or I die! This is a powerful idea that ties in closely with coming to peace in letting go. This doesn't mean, of course, that I am okay with them dying or me dying the next day. I am not okay with death, and, in fact, hate the prospect of it. Letting go simply means that I am satisfied with the interaction we had in this life. I am grateful for it, but I am simply done. I say thank you, goodbye, and good luck.

In this process, I am neither coming to peace with others dying nor with my own death. My genuine letting go is about managing the way I live with an eye on death. I do not need to accept death. That's exactly where the space of discomfort comes in.

My fear of death is a Gordian Knot that I feel I must deal with to move on. You could argue that I really don't need to answer the existential question of my own death because it's not answerable. You can manage aspects of the death experience through planning. You can also manage the fear of dying as with any other extreme feelings. But is that good enough? Maybe I'm not stretching my mind far enough on the subject. One way to go further is to reflect on my experience dealing with the idea of my death.

As I've already noted, I am an advanced cancer patient, and I get an imaging study done every six months to check the status of my disease. The past ten studies have been clear. But if the situation were different, I would be thinking of my death coming in about one or two years because the progression of my type of cancer can mean death within a few months to a couple of years. I always go to my surveillance test afraid of this possibility, and I live my life fearful of the outcome. It guts me. Dying in two years would mean my enjoyment of music would be cut short. I would not have time to see what book I might write after two years. And I wouldn't have the time to seek a new relationship, even if it ultimately meant experiencing another heartbreak.

As I listed my "potential losses," I realized that I already have had many of these experiences that I'm so worried about missing out on. Yes, I could lay the foundation for a new relationship, but I just enjoyed a fantastic love affair, and it ended. Do I really want one more heartbreak this badly? I have felt heartbreaks a few times in my life, and they were good. Looking back on my life, I can see that it has always been about meaningful experiences, and I've had plenty of those. Did I have enough? When can I say that I've had enough?

I started on this book after receiving my last cancer surveillance results. I have experienced the fear that precedes these tests and the worries about disease progression. I have also experienced the relief that comes when the results are good, as well as the fatigue that accompanies all these ups and downs.

I need to imagine the scenario of having only a short time to live. I would be rushing to finish my final projects, which are the three new manuscripts I'm working on that are at varying degrees of readiness. I am physically fine for the time being. I may want to spend more time with people, and I would laugh with them more. That is another of the challenges that this book addresses. I do not need to wait until I receive the news that I have only a few months to live before I start laughing more with the people I care about. I need to get into the mindset of fully living the experience as it unfolds and laughing as much as possible. I decided three books ago that I needed to laugh more, but it took a severe heartbreak to realize that I need to do that now.

LETTING GO OF ME. What is it that is me? How can I let go of myself? I have often felt too tired of trying to live. Living is hard. I could just let go of my desire to live. Why do I not end it all? I have also lived enough to realize that living involves suffering and pain. This pain I have endured in my heart is not pleasant. Life is not worth living if I have to continue in this agony and just get more. I could decide on my own to just end my life. Everyone has the means to do it. In my case, it's even easier. I could simply stop taking the medicine that's keeping me alive. Of course, there are faster ways to do it that I could use if I decide it's time to die. I want to die with dignity. I also do not want to suffer too much before I die.

After I went through the devastating end of a relationship, I started to relate more to those who find living unbearable after the loss of a loved one. Often that loss is the straw that breaks the camel's back, however, it may be the only inciting event. When I started writing this book, I felt the difficulty of regulating my emotions, and the agonizing pain I had inside pushed me to the edge. I wondered if it was worth it to carry on with this much pain. I present the following exercise for learning how to deal with this degree of pain.

This exercise is what I call suspending the commitment to self-regulating. It's the ultimate permission for you to disintegrate and hit rock bottom. Needless to say, finding the laughter to let go does not come to me from a space of joy. Instead, it comes from a space of struggle and a desire to escape. I am tired of living a painful experience but afraid that my struggle can tip me to the point of feeling that life isn't worth living. Regardless, I need to be able to encounter this possibility without succumbing to it. This takes me back to viewing humor as coming to the edge of a cliff and not jumping. Laughing can save me.

Therapy has taught me to challenge some of the essential notions I hold within me. Why would I not challenge those ideas that I have wanted to challenge? I want to challenge the desire to live and conform. I dream of death as getting lost in swirling winds that carry me into a dark substance. It's like falling endlessly. I think I am in a shitty place now. How would I know that dying is not worse? I am afraid of dying. I think I will be in a position of suffering for eternity. I could choose to die if I knew death is a place of peace where you just sleep and have no dreams. I worry that death is a state where the mind continues to suffer. I'd rather there be no mind. I hope there will be nothing that is "I"; otherwise, I wouldn't be released from my misery. Because of my fears, I want to not irreversibly go all the way. I want to be able to suspend judgment. This is what I call humor.

I am managing being alive. But what if death will take me into spaces where there is nothing I can control? But why do I always need to worry about control? This is when laughter becomes my antidote. I need to give up the control by laughing.

Letting go with laughter is liberation

I said that I live to laugh and I choose to let go. But how do I reconcile that with my desire to build my life and live it to the fullest? Actually, I don't need to reconcile it. Part of my life choice is to let go of the need to reconcile anything. There is tension between wanting to let go and wanting to live. There is something inauthentic about it. It's like you're letting go of what you cannot manage or regulate. You're laughing at what you can't get access to. It's problematic. At the same time, I feel like this notion is necessary. It's pertinent to reconcile with the desire to continue living.

I want to explore what insanity means. Not in the sense of doing drugs or living on the street, but rather of countering some of my foundational assumptions about this world. One example is the idea of "being authentic!"

The rational in me wants me to be authentic to myself. But I laugh at this idea, as by changing who I am, being authentic to my old self is meaningless. Since I am constantly changing, the idea of being authentic seems like nonsense. Obviously, this is a silly idea that I do not believe, but I will pursue it.

The rationale is that you have an expectation of what takes place in your life, including what that should be and who you are. Then, events happen, and you move on. The irrational is the continued pursuit of futile efforts. It's the desire that's never going to be fulfilled. It's keeping on with that heaviness on your chest and not struggling to get out from under it. It's following that which has no meaning.

Humor is ingenious; it occurs between honesty and lies and is distinct from both. You can be honest, you can lie to hide, or you can exploit humor to attain other ends. Those ends are legitimate or not. Humor is powerful and dangerous, which is why I am drawn to exploring it. Humor allows you to test the limits and experiment. It channels the whims and impulses and puts them in a place where you are still safe to be or not to be who you are. It's the "to not be" in Hamlet's question, and to me, that's the more original answer.

Noncontradiction is important for me. But do I have to not be self-contradictory? I contradict myself all the time. Do I really believe that when I thought I wasn't contradicting myself, I actually wasn't? I live my life managing my contradictions and packaging stuff around them so that they don't bother me. I can give up this desire not to be self-contradictory.

Five years ago, I thought I was going to die imminently and stopped any productive activity. But I am still alive. In the meantime, I have contributed what I could and worked harder than I imagined. I am tired of working this hard and maybe it's time for me to rest. I am also not sure about what impact my work will have. I cannot put my finger on where I am putting the most meaning in my life.

If I want to continue living and hopefully leaving an impact, I need to optimize my situation to continue to be me (or not be me) in pursuing my efforts. I could also explore other modes of expression besides writing, such as music, singing, and poetry. I could develop these tools more so that I could use them better. Maybe learning how to laugh is a contribution I am making to this world—teaching others how to laugh and let go. Perhaps it can liberate someone who is stuck.

I have freed myself by laughing and letting go; maybe someone else will do the same.

Planning to laugh and let go

We can look back at an experience and decide to let go and laugh about it. But can we also plan for an experience and be intentional about laughing and letting go during it? Yes, we can plan to laugh. Try launching an interaction with laughter. You might laugh at something you've seen and begin the conversation in that way before you even say hello. It's probably best to not tell a joke right at the beginning. A quick one-sentence story followed by laughter will be enough. A broad smile can also be enough. And if the other person smiles, you can both laugh. I think greeting someone else with laughter communicates warmth. Be watchful of the other person's response, however. If you're laughing and they're frowning, it could lead to a disconnection. Stay on the same wavelength. Try to laugh at a scheduled time and then laugh outside of a schedule. Remind yourself that you live to laugh, and live by your mantra. Laughter is to be lived in every action.

To laugh, be attentive to the funny, ridiculous, and ironic. Develop a framework for capturing what is comical. Calling out someone's anxiety with laughter is funny. It's a tease, but it's a safe one. A little flirting and laughter are fine, if appropriate. Warm remarks are good. Do not throw anyone under the bus, and do not make someone the object of your laughter when you are with others. Don't poke fun at anyone's insecurities, unless they're okay with that. Comment on what's outside that can be funny and laugh at and with it.

Laughter isn't always about the content; it's about the experience. Capture and be present in the moment. Listen. Observe. Laugh.

Move toward a serious conversation and then retreat. It's a good idea to break the tension with laughter after a serious conversation. Laugh with the others who are participating. Don't do what you know you will feel heavy or guilty about later. Take risks but apologize if you overdo it. Move on. Don't hold the thought in your mind for too long. Let go of your expectations of how things should be before an experience, and keep an open mind instead. You can imagine how things might go, however. Push your creativity further into realms that you haven't experienced before. Don't get stuck repeating what you know. Respond to another person's offers. Initiate offerings. Manage your emotions so that you stay in the present. And don't worry about what will happen afterwards.

Trust me, you will have a good time.

Letting go of letting go

This book is my boldest attempt to obtain self-liberation. I needed to let go of my avoidance of the crazy, so I chose to let it out. I needed to laugh at my obsession with being rational and reasonable. I didn't want to come to terms with daunting subjects such as death, fear, and sadness. I didn't want to accept them. And I hated dealing with my suffering using inauthentic gratitude. I refuse to be a puppet exuding positivity while being in deep shit. I also cannot just accept the nonsense of life as okay; I am not someone who likes to surrender. That's why I decided to laugh.

I want to reconcile myself with insanity. I am giving up the need to be consistent. I take in and accept contradictions at a deeper existential level. I laugh at this. I insist that I want to be authentic while enduring my struggles and living with love. Yet, I liberate myself from whatever holds me back. I am often in tremendous pain inside. It hurts. Living is hard, and continuing to participate with authenticity and love is daunting. I am experiencing the intensity of the desire for things I cannot attain. I feel the pressure of having to hold it together, and I don't want that anymore. It's in this space of suffering that I hover. I want to be able to break apart without breaking apart.

I still want to have the experience of mental pain and heartache because I hope to turn these agonies into opportunities for deeper self-actualization. Laughter and humor are always available to set me free to manage what I confront while living a constraining reality. I create more space between me and the worlds I am living. I am experiencing the desire to care to even want something. With my pain, I lack the will to want. I laugh at that and continue to hold my desire. I realize a voice coming from my sucky reality telling me I should stop. I ache. Then, I find something to laugh at and move on. I heal and then choose to participate again. At times, all I can do is to protect myself from the moral damage of witnessing the pain of others. I laugh to celebrate our resiliency and move on.

There is also the "Letting Go," capitalized, that takes place when you push the exercise of laughing and letting go to its limit. You're down to the bare metal. You've let go of it all, and now you're empty.

How can I laugh when I don't feel anything? I am numb. I laugh at the nothingness. I have steps for addressing this state. Begin with laughing. Laugh by moving the air through your lungs and stretching the muscles on your face. Laugh again and again. Sit with the experience and think of how you're experiencing the nothingness. I am experiencing the void as a slowness in my brain. I feel like my brain is an empty white space or a page with only a few words that are not linked to each other. I cannot hear the voices in my head. From the outside, I hear the noise of the objects surrounding me. I hear the fan and the sound of my dog's flicking tongue after enjoying his meal. Actually, I'm not sure the word "enjoy" is valid here. My dog gobbles up his meals so quickly that it doesn't seem he has the time to actually enjoy them. But do I really "enjoy" things when I think I do? Why is speed a factor? I describe these so-called enjoyable events here as only experiences. I feel the silence in the room and the noise that my fingers make on the keyboard. But outside of that, there is nothing.

My dog moves around in the room again, and I hear the scratching of his nails on the wood floor. I've latched on to things again. Now, I am more grounded, and my mind begins to fill up. I also start to find some little irony/humor/joke in what's around me. The irony is that as I was complaining about the emptiness, my awareness began to fill up with stuff, some of it new. I heard sounds I didn't hear before. I also felt feelings that I hadn't captured earlier, and I enjoyed them, too. I became aware of the present moment, my moment to enjoy. I can recall the experience as I felt it in that specific moment. I don't mind living this way, and I don't mind this sense of "emptiness." If I continue living this way, I think my life will be okay.

I want to emphasize that I am speaking of laughter and letting go from a place of misery. But I am not dead, nor am I giving up on living. In fact, the opposite is true: I am *very much alive*. I am driven to live fully and for as long as I can. So what will I gain from laughing and letting go? I will earn a free soul. I can choose what I am bothered by rather than allow whatever is happening to bother me. When I get upset, I will choose the scale and extent to which I will be disturbed. In doing so, I will gain a light heart that's not weighed down by the ghosts of the past. I can search with my soul and go places I choose to go to. My next step is to determine what I have control over.

I ask myself, "What will you do next?" I am troubled by world problems, as many of us are, but I know I can't solve them. I can participate in helping to alleviate some of these problems, and I have the tools for participation. But the universe is hypercomplex, and my contribution is minimal, at best. I can write a book or ten and make music to brighten someone's mood. My hope is that people will feel their hearts warm through my words and be inspired to connect with others. I am certainly not in the place to create a whole system that will change the world. Who is? I am barely managing to survive and move on with laughter.

I think of the dreams I have set myself to work toward. I ask myself, are they worthy? Are they reachable in my lifetime? If not, does the work I do contribute to their achievement in any meaningful way? I have set the pursuit of justice as the purpose of my life's project. If I lived another 50 years, I would want my contribution to be toward the attainment of social justice. Do I still want that now? Yes, I believe I do.

I don't want to give up pursuing justice. I carry on laughing at the tension that comes with the anxiety of this letting go. I don't want to let go of justice, in the sense of fairness, as a guiding value and as a pursuit. As a matter of fact, I am writing this book intending to share it so that others can pursue their own projects with lighter loads. In that sense, I can foresee my work here contributing to justice. I want justice, and that's precisely why I am doing what I am at this specific moment. In my situation, I genuinely believe that the best thing I can do at this time is to write this book. The bottom line is that I am writing to make existence more tolerable for those who are tormented like me. In my mind, there is the hope that if they laugh more and develop the bandwidth to manage their lives, they can better tackle the issues related to social justice. But this is simply my hope; I have no guarantees.

It's true that my tools are finite, that I am finite. Can justice, in the sense of fairness, be achieved in 50 years? I'm not sure, but I will pursue it with a leap of faith. I laugh at my persistence.

Let me push my mind a little bit further. I want justice because I care for others. But do I really enjoy caring for others? I care for others I know personally with whom I have an emotional connection. I care for children, and when I see someone in pain, I want to lessen their pain. I do not necessarily enjoy every concrete act of care toward every single person. But that's not what matters. What matters to me is that people suffer less. I would rather I didn't have to participate in alleviating suffering, so I play more music and sing. However, it is truly essential to me that people suffer less, so I take it as a duty to participate and help in whatever way I can.

Why would I not let go of caring? I don't want to let go of caring. I enjoy others' well-being and want participating toward it to be a fundamental part of what I do. That is truly meaningful to me. "Well, you enjoy it," you might say, "but what else do you enjoy more than caring?" Well, when you put it that way, I have to admit that I enjoy singing more than caring. Singing and music give me more pleasure. I also enjoy sharing my artwork after I've developed it well. I enjoy working on what gives me joy, and this motivates me to develop my expressions in an exemplary way that will inspire others who are similarly seeking. Most of all, I enjoy working in an expressive area that I am passionate about.

My areas of passion involve writing, music, and singing. The activity has to have an expressive component, so that I can share what is essential to me. But here is another aspect: working on my duties also gives me joy and pleasure. I am happier when I contribute something meaningful to others. I also become miserable and feel empty when I only pursue my own desires and passions. This is a new realization. Maybe finding the perfect balance between working in my areas of passion and my calling or duty will give me the right amount of joy and fulfillment. That would be an optimal state. When I am working on what I love, I can be creative and artful. I am talented in that, and it brings me joy. Masterfully using my skills in the service of duty also gives me pleasure. This means using words to express meaning and make sense of human struggles and other experiences. It's not that much different from using music to heal myself and helping others heal by infusing our experience with enjoyment and joy.

I am going to do just that. I will find the right balance between what I consider my duty and what I define as my passion and art. I have tipped one way or the other along the way. Maybe it is time to laugh at my enthusiasm and find balance in the middle ground.

Before thinking about my life ahead and where to invest my time, I want to further explore this idea of passion. I am specifically curious about my passion for doing creative work. You may ask, "Is there any other passion?" Let's elaborate a little on passion. What is a passion? It's the space that makes your heart race with excitement. It's the space in which you can't get enough. You go to sleep because you worry you'll be tired the next day, but you wish you could just carry on. For me, my passion is to create meaning in whatever I choose to do. I am creating meaning here. How can I expound on the notion of passion sufficiently so that I can reproduce it? Now that I have realized what passion is, I need to go back to the central question of this book—life and its meaning.

At this point, we are ready to think about life and the time we have left on this planet. Think of three categories of projects you can work on in your lifetime. There is a project that stems from your passion. There is also a project that is your duty. And finally, there is a project that sustains your daily needs. It's ideal if you can combine all three. However, that is most often not the case and will probably never be unless you're missing something in the definition and not allowing yourself to name your true passions or duties. I worry about people whose passion is fulfilling their duties! They have often failed to develop other aspects of their personalities, such as art and self-expression. If your obsessions are always with the world of facts, you're missing community, relationship, and humanness. If you say that you love people and enjoy them, and that they are your sole passion, I remind you that the world of ideas is beautiful too, and there is a lot of space there to explore. There are also many bodily pleasures to get in touch with and enjoy. Maybe with your obsession with loving and serving people, you have forgotten some of your own joys in life.

The third category, working to make ends meet, is something that needs to be named. Part of what we do is necessary for living. For example, I need health insurance, so I cannot just quit my job and run away.

Now that we have delineated the three main categories, we can add a fourth to include everything else. I call this fourth category the "everything else," for simplicity. This category includes those items that have accumulated over time, things that you were passionate about at some point but no longer have an interest in. It may contain those things that you needed to sustain a living for but no longer need or things that you felt a sense of duty toward for a while but no longer do.

You need to look at where you're spending your time every day within these four categories and have the flexibility to say, "No, this is not what I want to do." What applies to work also applies to your relationships. Suppose I am focused on building a new relationship and forget about my old ones. In this case, I won't be able to sustain them. At the same time, when looking at the old relationships, you need to be selective about what you consider essential and what you can spend less time engaging in. You need to have the space to seek out and identify new connections. We all need to renew our energy and our lives, and we grow when there are new people around us.

There is a meaningful sense of community that comes when we connect with others. Of course, people can be at particular points in their lives that differ from where you are. What you want from a relationship can differ from what the other person wants. Be open to possibilities and don't take their position and what they do personally. The key here, obviously, is managing the feelings that can trigger you to go in one direction or the other. I learned from my last relationship that I am capable of being ungraceful and that I struggle to let go. I also knew that I could be grateful. That's one reason I wrote this book, so that I could learn to live more with grace and kindness. Still, it's my duty alone to pursue how I define my passions and then commit to spending my life working on them.

But what does all of this have to do with justice? Laughter is available equally to every person, while therapy is not. Moreover, finding a therapist who won't cause you more trauma is not easy. Anyone can laugh at any moment. Laughter is liberating. And you can change your position if you choose to laugh. You can break free from where you were stuck. Through humor, you can see other perspectives yet realize that you don't have to be what others want. It's not only about being stoic; it's also about finding laughter and joy. People who are suffering need laughter more than ever. In this increasingly complex world, they have more things to laugh about and more triggers for their feelings of disappointment. They have a greater need to heal, and there is more and more material they can use to help them heal through laughter. The struggle is abundantly rich.

Laughing is the greatest equalizer. This work is for the poor and miserable among us. Do the privileged also need to heal through laughter, or do I want them to suffer? I do not wish for anyone to suffer, really. Maybe if they heal, they will stop making others suffer. Maybe if billionaire jerks discover they can laugh and experience joy, that it is within them, they won't be so preoccupied with owning and dominating. Maybe they'll stop oppressing others. Oppression is an attempt to beat down someone else and to steal their laughter. The oppressor wants to steal laughter from others; they want the joy to be for them alone, but they define joy as the possession of objects. They take from others so they can enjoy their distinction and status. Fuck them.

Letting go is a way to move on and try again. If you feel beaten down by life, carrying on requires that you think about your options and find ways out. You need to decide where you will focus the energy you do have to move forward. Many will have to make difficult decisions. People will struggle, get stuck, and stagnate. Getting stuck is, in many ways, the antithesis to becoming lighter through laughter. Everyone can laugh and make others laugh. Sharing laughter can feed your spirit to keep going. So find your audience and laugh with them.

Don't allow yourself to stay stuck. Live to laugh and let go!

Made in the USA
Middletown, DE
28 October 2022

13654764R00066